Introduction

What is Oxford Living Grammar?

Oxford Living Grammar is a series of three books which explain and practise grammar in **everyday contexts**. They show how grammar is used in **real-life situations** that learners themselves will experience. The books can be used for self-study, for homework, and in class.

Elementary: CEF level A1+ (towards KET level)

Pre-intermediate: CEF level A2 (KET and towards PET level)

Intermediate: CEF level B1 (PET and towards FCE level)

How are the books organized?

The books are divided into four-page units, each of which deals with an important grammar topic. Units are divided into two two-page parts. Each unit begins with an explanation of the grammar point, and includes a unique **Grammar in action** section which shows how the grammar is used in typical everyday situations. It explains **when** to use the grammar point. This is followed by a number of **contextualized exercises** for learners to practise the grammar they have read about. The second part of each unit introduces additional explanation of the topic, more Grammar in action, and more contextualized exercises. The last exercise in every unit provides practice of a variety of the points and contexts introduced across the four pages.

The intention is that the fully contextualized explanations and exercises will show real English in real situations, which learners can recognize and apply to their own experience.

Word focus boxes highlight unfamiliar words or expressions and enable learners to widen their vocabulary.

The **Over to you** section at the back of the book provides a **comprehensive bank of review exercises**. Learners are encouraged to do more creative tasks about themselves and their own experience, using what they have learned. Sample answers are provided for these tasks.

There is an *Oxford Living Grammar* **Context-Plus CD-ROM** at each level with further grammar practice and Word focus exercises. Learners can also build longer texts, and build and take part in dialogues; learners can record and listen to their own voice to improve pronunciation. There are six grammar tests at each level so learners can see if there are any areas they would like to study again.

What grammar is included?

At Intermediate level, you will study all the grammar necessary for Cambridge PET and much of the grammar required for the FCE. The choice of contexts in the exercises has been informed by the Common European Framework of Reference and the framework of the Association of Language Testers in Europe at B1.

How can students use Oxford Living Grammar on their own?

You can work through the book from beginning to end. All the units will present and practise the grammar in typical everyday situations. When you have finished the exercises, you can go to the Over to you tasks for that topic at the back of the book for extra practice, and then check your answers.

Or when you have a particular grammar problem, you might want to study that topic first. You can look up the topic you need in the Contents at the front of the book, or in the Index at the back.

How can teachers use the material in the classroom?

Oxford Living Grammar enables your students to learn and practise English grammar in context. The contexts are typical everyday situations that your students themselves will experience, such as talking about their own experiences, having conversations with people they have met, talking about other people, and discussing common topics.

The syllabus is divided into 30 four-page units, which we hope will make the book ideal for study over an academic year. Units can be studied in any order, or you and your students can work through the book from beginning to end. The Over to you tasks provide freer practice and more creative review tasks.

Contents

iate

n Coe

OXFORD
UNIVERSITY PRESS

OXFORD
UNIVERSITY PRESS

Great Clarendon Street, Oxford OX2 6DP

Oxford University Press is a department of the University of Oxford.
It furthers the University's objective of excellence in research, scholarship,
and education by publishing worldwide in

Oxford New York

Auckland Cape Town Dar es Salaam Hong Kong Karachi
Kuala Lumpur Madrid Melbourne Mexico City Nairobi
New Delhi Shanghai Taipei Toronto

With offices in

Argentina Austria Brazil Chile Czech Republic France Greece
Guatemala Hungary Italy Japan Poland Portugal Singapore
South Korea Switzerland Thailand Turkey Ukraine Vietnam

OXFORD and OXFORD ENGLISH are registered trade marks of
Oxford University Press in the UK and in certain other countries

ISBN: 978 0 19 455707 8 Student's Book
ISBN: 978 0 19 455708 5 Student's CD-ROM Pack

Printed in China

ACKNOWLEDGEMENTS

Illustrations by: Tim Bradford/Illustration Ltd pp 2, 3, 4, 5, 6, 8, 10, 11,, 12, 13,
14, 16, 18, 19, 20, 21, 22, 24, 26, 27, 28, 32, 34, 36, 37, 38, 40, 42, 44, 45, 46,
48, 50, 51, 52, 53, 54, 56, 58, 59, 60, 61, 62, 64, 66, 67, 68, 69, 70, 72, 74, 77, 78,
80, 83, 84, 85, 86, 90, 91, 93, 94, 96, 98, 100, 101, 102, 106, 107, 108, 109, 112,
114, 116, 118, 119, 120, 121; Ian Whadcock/Eastwing pp 9, 17, 23, 25, 31, 41,
47, 49, 55, 57, 63, 65, 71, 73, 81, 87, 88, 95, 105.

Cover image: Darwin Wiggett/Digital Vision/Getty Images

*We would also like to thank the following for permission to reproduce the following
photographs and other copyright material*: Alamy pp 33 (floods/Jeff Morgan
Environmental Issues), 43 (A Flemming/Mary Evans Picture Library, A Bolt/
Aflo Foto Agency), 79 (cars/Ken Welsh), 89 (Sagrada Familia/Imagebroker); The
Bridgeman Art Library p 29 (Portrait of a Bearded Man, c113, Vinci, Leonardo
da (1452-1519)/Biblioteca Reale, Turin, Italy), (Design for a Scythed Chariot
and Armoured Car, c1487, Vinci, Leonardo da (1452-1519)/British Museum,
London UK), 113 (Self Portrait with Velvet Dress, 1926, Kahlo, Frida (1910-54)/
Private Collection/Photo: Jorge Contreras Chacel); Picture Library UK p 115
(omelette/Amanda Heywood/Fresh food Images); Rex Features p 7 (Olympic
Celebrations/Sipa Press); OUP pp 15 (New York/Image 100), 39 (Portrait girl/
Imageshop), 43 (Sphinx/Photodisc).

Adjectives and adverbs

Prepositions

Building sentences

01 Present simple and present continuous
Forms, uses, and contexts

1 Present simple

Here are some examples of the **present simple**:

> We **live** in a house but Jim **lives** in a flat.
> Rod **doesn't like** beer and I **don't like** it, either.
> **Do** you **speak** French? **Does** Terry **speak** Dutch?

We add **-s** to the positive **he/she/it** form of regular verbs. (For more information on irregular verbs, see p. 127.)

We use **do/does** in negatives and questions.

2 We use the **present simple** to talk about permanent situations, facts, and regular, repeated, or constant actions:

> The River Amazon **flows** into the Atlantic.
> They **don't have** school on Saturdays.
> Where **do** you **live**? **Does** she **work** here?

3 Present continuous

We form the **present continuous** with the present of **be (am/is/are) + the -ing form**.

> What **is** Sara **doing**? ~ She's **studying** for her exams.

(For rules on spelling the *-ing* form, see p. 127.)

4 We use the **present continuous** to talk about something happening at or around the moment of speaking:

> Jane can't come to the phone — she's **having** a bath.

5 We use the **present continuous** for an incomplete action or situation:

> Jim lives near me, but this week he's **staying** with his parents.

6 Some verbs describe states and do not normally have continuous tenses:

> I **like** Spanish films. (NOT I'm liking Spanish films.)

We use state verbs to talk about thoughts (e.g. **believe, know, seem, think, understand**), feelings (e.g. **agree, hope, like, love, want**), existence (**be**), possession (e.g. **have, belong, own**), and the properties of something (e.g. **cost, contain, include, mean**).

> TIP
Note that some verbs can describe an action or state, e.g.:

> Do you **have** a car? (state)
> She's **having** a shower. (action now)
> She **has** a shower every morning. (regular action)

> The food **looks** good. (state)
> What are they **looking** at? (action now)
> I always **look** at the sports pages. (regular action)

> John **is** 12 years old. (state)
> John **is being** naughty. (action now)
> John **is** often naughty. (regular action)

Grammar in action

1 We can use the **present simple** to talk about where people live, study, and work:

> My husband, Jack, and I **live** in Leeds but I **work** in Bradford.

2 We use the **present simple** for things we do every day or most days:

> Do you **watch** the news on TV? ~ No, I don't usually **get** home in time but I often **listen** to the news on the radio before I go to sleep.

We often use frequency adverbs (*often, usually*, etc.) with the present simple.

3 We use the **present simple** to explain how we do things, or how things happen in business, politics, science, etc.:

> How do I **make** an omelette? Well, I **break** two eggs into a bowl, I **add** a little salt …
> Water **freezes** at 0°C and **boils** at 100°C.

4 We use the **present continuous** to talk about things that have started but not finished, for example when we describe our current situation in letters, emails, etc.:

> We're **staying** in a lovely hotel by the sea. We're **being** very lazy, and getting up late every day.

The actions and situations we describe are not always in progress at this **exact** moment. Here, someone talks about their life **around** the moment of speaking:

> I'm very busy – I'm **spending** most of my time looking after my son, but I'm also **learning** Italian and I'm **taking** my accountancy exams.

A A fire-fighter doesn't only fight fires

Complete the text by using the verbs in brackets in the present simple.

Naturally, fire-fighters ___put___ [0] (put) out fires, but their job also _____ [1] (include) many other things. They often _____ [2] (rescue) people from car crashes, and when there is a flood, they _____ [3] (pump) the water out of buildings. And they _____ always _____ [4] (not, work) with humans. If someone _____ [5] (phone) to say that their cat is stuck in a tree, the fire service _____ [6] (send) someone to save it. In some places, a fire-fighter _____ [7] (not, work) 8 hours every day. Instead, they _____ [8] (do) a 24-hour shift and then _____ [9] (have) two days off – which of course _____ [10] (equal) 8 hours a day!

B What are the children doing?

A father phones home to talk to the babysitter. Complete the conversation with the present continuous of the verbs in the box. Use short forms where possible.

> ask be behave build concentrate do
> draw help look ~~phone~~ sit talk try

SAM   Hello, Ann. This is Sam. I _'m phoning_ [0] to ask about the children. I'm glad that you _____ [1] after them, but _____ they _____ [2] well?

ANN   Oh, yes. They are _____ [3] very good.

SAM   What _____ Jimmy _____ [4]?

ANN   He _____ [5] a bridge on the floor with his Lego.

SAM   And _____ Laura _____ [6] him?

ANN   No, she _____ [7] at the table. She _____ [8] to draw a tiger.

LAURA   Who _____ you _____ [9] to, Ann?

ANN   It's your father. He _____ [10] about you. Do you want to talk to him?

LAURA   No, just tell him that I _____ [11] a picture for him and I _____ [12] very hard.

C Canteen conversation

Some office workers are talking at lunchtime. Complete the conversation by crossing out the form that doesn't fit.

TIM   I see that you *'re eating / eat* [0] a vegetarian dish. *Are / Do* you always *eating / eat* [0] vegetarian food?

CLAIRE   No, I *'m eating / eat* [1] everything, but I *'m trying / try* [2] this today because it *'s looking / looks* [3] so good.

TIM   My cousin is a vegan. That *'s meaning / means* [4] that he *isn't eating / doesn't eat* [5] any animal products. At the moment he *'s suffering / suffers* [6] from a vitamin problem and the doctor *'s thinking / thinks* [7] that he should eat some fish or meat.

FRED   It *'s seeming / seems* [8] silly to me to be so strict. People *aren't killing / don't kill* [9] animals to get milk or eggs, for example.

TIM   I *'m agreeing / agree* [10] with you, but my cousin *'s believing / believes* [11] that we shouldn't exploit animals at all.

CLAIRE   Well, I *'m hoping / hope* [12] that he'll soon get over his vitamin problem.

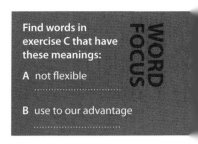

WORD FOCUS

Find words in exercise C that have these meanings:

A   not flexible

_____

B   use to our advantage

_____

Present simple and present continuous
Present tenses with future meaning

7 We can use the **present simple** and the **present continuous** to talk about the future:

> The exam **starts** at 9.00 and **lasts** 3 hours.
> I**'m meeting** Ellie tomorrow night – we**'re going** to the cinema to see the new Coen brothers film.

Grammar in action

5 We use the **present simple** to talk about something in the future that is **officially organized**, for example on a timetable or schedule:

> The hotel will provide a packed lunch because the coach leaves at 7.30 and doesn't return until the evening.
> What date do classes start next term? ~ Term starts on 15th September but classes don't start until a week later.

6 We use the **present continuous** to talk about something in the future that we have agreed to do:

> Tim and I are going to the theatre tonight, then we're having dinner at White's.

Here, we are talking about our plans for the weekend:

> Are you doing anything at the weekend? ~ I'm playing tennis with Mary on Saturday.

D   Making arrangements to travel

A boss is talking to his secretary. Use the verbs in brackets to complete the dialogue with the present simple. Use short forms where possible.

BOSS   Remind me of the arrangements for tomorrow, Robin.

ROBIN   Well, your flight <u>departs</u> ⁰ (depart) from Heathrow at 7.10.

BOSS   OK. And which terminal _____ it _____ ¹ (leave) from?

ROBIN   It _____ ² (leave) from Terminal 2. You _____ ³ (not / arrive) in Frankfurt until 9.40, then you _____ ⁴ (take) the shuttle bus into town.

BOSS   9.40?

ROBIN   Yes, the flight _____ ⁵ (last) an hour and a half but Germany is one hour ahead.

BOSS   Oh, yes, of course. And the meetings? When _____ they _____ ⁶ (begin)?

ROBIN   At 11.00. After the meetings you _____ ⁷ (have) plenty of time for lunch because your flight back _____ ⁸ (not / leave) until 6 o'clock. It _____ ⁹ (get) back here at 6.30 local time.

BOSS   That's fine because there _____ ¹⁰ (be) a Champions League match tomorrow but it _____ ¹¹ (not / start) until quarter to eight.

E Arranging to meet

Use a verb from the box in the present simple or the present continuous to complete the dialogue. Use short forms where possible.

begin	do	not do	get	go	go	leave	not leave	meet	take

EMMA There's an interesting talk on healthy living at the library this Friday. I'm ...going... [0] with Sarah. We .... [1] in the café opposite. How about joining us?

JACK What time .... it .... [2]?

EMMA At 7 o'clock.

JACK I .... [3] my brother to the station on Friday and his train .... [4] until about quarter to seven so I won't be back in time, I'm afraid. What about the weekend? .... you .... [5] anything special on Saturday?

EMMA Yes, lots of us .... [6] to the anti-war demonstration in Leeds.

JACK How .... you .... [7] there?

EMMA In Sarah's car. We .... [8] her flat at 9.00. I'm sure there's room for you.

JACK OK, I .... [9] anything else, so I'll join you.

F Making excuses

Look at Alan's diary for next week and then read the email messages he has received. Use the words given to write his replies.

Monday 7 p.m. Dinner with Mary.
Tuesday 4.30 p.m. Tennis with Peter
Thursday p.m. Help Sam with move

Friday 1 p.m. Lunch with the boss
Saturday a.m. Shopping with mum

0 Alan: Do you want to go to the cinema on Monday evening? Lenny

Hi, Lenny. Monday evening / no good. I / have / dinner with Mary. How about Wednesday?

Hi, Lenny. *Monday evening is no good. I'm having dinner with Mary.* How about Wednesday?

1 Alan: Can we meet on Tuesday afternoon to talk about the holiday? Sue

Hi Sue. I / afraid / can't meet on Tuesday afternoon because I / play / tennis with Peter. Alan

Hi Sue. .... Alan

2 Hi Alan. Any chance of seeing you on Thursday afternoon? Kim

Kim: I / sorry / can't / see you on Thursday afternoon. I / help / Sam move into his new flat. Alan

Kim: .... Alan

3 Dear Alan: Can we have lunch together on Friday? Love, Mum

Dear Mum, Friday / no good. I / have / lunch / with the boss. Anyway, I / see / you on Saturday. Love, Alan

Dear Mum, ... Love, Alan

4 Hi Alan: Are you free on Saturday morning? I need your advice. Tony

Hi Tony. Sorry, I / go / shopping / with my mum on Saturday morning. you / do / anything in the evening? Alan

Hi Tony. .... Alan

OVER TO YOU Now go to page 122.

1 Past simple
To form the positive **past simple**, add **-ed** to the verb. We form negatives and questions with **did/didn't +** **verb**:

*Last Saturday I **painted** my bedroom.*
*Ella **didn't stay** at the party very long.* (NOT ~~didn't stayed~~)
***Did** you **enjoy** your birthday?* (NOT ~~did you enjoyed~~)

The past simple is the same in all persons. Many common verbs are irregular.
(For more information, see p. 129.)

2 We use the **past simple** to talk about:

- short events in the past:
  *When **did** Oscar **phone** you?*

- longer past actions:
  *Mary and Tim **studied** physics at university.*

- repeated events in the past:
  *Dr. Thomas **visited** 43 patients yesterday.*

- past states:
  *Computers **cost** much more a few years ago.*

3 We often use the **past simple** with time expressions such as **yesterday, last week/year, in 1999, two years ago, when?, how long?**:

***Did** the accident **happen** yesterday or several days ago?*
*When **did** they **move**? ~ They **moved** in 2007.*
*How long **did** you **stay**? ~ We **stayed** for two years.*

5 Past continuous
We form the **past continuous** with **was/were + -ing** form:

*They **were waiting** for a bus.*
*It **wasn't raining** at the time.*
***Were** you **listening** to me?*

6 We use the **past continuous** to describe an action or situation in the past that continued for a period of time:

*It **was snowing** heavily all that day.*
*She **was crying** while watching the film.*

7 We can use the **past continuous** for two actions that were both in progress at the same time:

*While I **was cleaning** the floors, the children **were washing** the windows.*

Grammar in action

1 We use the **past simple** to talk about completed actions in the past. We often mention **when** the action happened. We can build up a picture of the past, for example at an interview:

INTERVIEWER	*When did you finish school?*
BETH	*I finished in 1999.*
INTERVIEWER	*Did you go to university in the same year?*
BETH	*No. First, I went abroad for a year. I worked in an orphanage in Mexico. I stayed there for six months.*

2 We use the **past continuous** to talk about actions we were in the middle of at particular times in the past:

POLICEMAN	*What were you doing yesterday at 6 o' clock?*
MAN	*I was visiting my grandmother.*
POLICEMAN	*We know that you made a phone call from your car at 6.15. Where were you going when you made that call?*
MAN	*I was going home.*

3 We use the **past simple** to give the actions in a story, and we use the **past continuous** to give background information about the situation:

It was raining so Mrs Tailor put on her coat. The children were waiting by the door. She kissed them and set off for the station. While she was waiting for the train, she noticed a handbag under a bench.

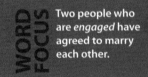
A At the time it happened

We often ask what people were doing when something important happened. Complete these questions and answers by writing in the correct form of the verbs given.

MIRA   What <u>were you doing</u> ⁰ (you, do) when you <u>heard</u> ⁰ (hear) that London would host the Olympics in 2012?

PETRA   Strangely enough, I ....¹ (spend) some time with friends in
         England. After a couple of days in Liverpool, we ....² (set) off
         for the south. We ....³ (reach) London in the late morning of
         the very day that they ....⁴ (make) the announcement, but of
         course the celebrations ....⁵ (not, start) until the afternoon.
         When we ....⁶ (arrive) in Greenwich in south London we
         ....⁷ (not, plan) to stay, but the sun ....⁸
         (shine) and everyone ....⁹ (walk) up and down because there
         was a special festival. Anyway, we ....¹⁰ (decide) to join in the
         fun. Just before 1 p.m., while we ....¹¹ (have) an ice cream
         in the park, the band that ....¹² (play) music for the dancing
         ....¹³ (stop) in the middle of the song and the bandleader
         ....¹⁴ (announce) that London had won the 2012 Olympics! The
         news really ....¹⁵ (add) to the party atmosphere, of course.

ED   Where ....¹⁶ (you, be) when the tsunami disaster
         ....¹⁷ (happen)?
AMY   I ....¹⁸ (lie) in bed because I ....¹⁹ (have)
         flu. I ....²⁰ (watch) an old film on television, although I
         ....²¹ (not, enjoy) it very much because I ....²²
         (not, think) it was very good. Then suddenly they ....²³
         (interrupt) the programme to give the news.

DAVE   What ....²⁴ (you, do) when you ....²⁵ (hear) that
         your sister was engaged?
CLAIRE   I ....²⁶ (walk) to work and I ....²⁷ (get) a text
         message on my mobile. My sister ....²⁸ (send) me a photo of
         her hand, and she ....²⁹ (wear) an engagement ring! At first
         I ....³⁰ (not, believe) the news, but then I ....³¹
         (call) her and she ....³² (tell) me the good news herself!

B   Rose's email

**Complete Rose's email to a friend about her busy weekend. Choose the correct form
of the verbs given.**

Dear Jessica,

Thanks for the email that you *sent/~~were sending~~*⁰ last Friday. I *didn't have/wasn't having*¹ time to reply at the
weekend because Mike and I *spent/were spending*² most of the time doing jobs in the flat. First, of course,
we *had/were having*³ to go to the shops to buy all the things we needed, then we *started/were starting*⁴
work. Mike *had/was having*⁵ a small accident while we *worked/were working*⁶. I *painted/was painting*⁷ and
he *put/was putting*⁸ up some new shelves when he *fell/was falling*⁹ off the ladder. He *didn't be/wasn't being*¹⁰
careful. We *worked/were working*¹¹ hard both days, and *didn't finish/weren't finishing*¹² everything until
Sunday evening. What *did you do/were you doing*¹³ at the weekend? *Did you see/Were you seeing*¹⁴ the film
that you *mentioned/were mentioning*¹⁵ in your email? Who *did you go/were you going*¹⁶ with?

Write soon,

Rose

---

8 Notice the forms of **used to**:

> *My cousin **used to** be a boy scout.*
> *I **didn't use to** like chocolate.*
> ***Did** they **use to** cause trouble at school?*

9 We use **used to** for past habits and regular past activities:

> *Ian **used to** swim every week.* (= He doesn't swim every week now.)
> ***Did** Sara **use to** take piano lessons?*

10 We also use **used to** for situations in the past that continued for some time:

> ***Did** there **use to** be a cinema here?*
> *Liz **used to** live in Highgate.* (= Liz doesn't live in Highgate now.)

> We often use the negative form **never used to**, as a more informal way of saying 'didn't use to':
> *Our daughter never used to wear make-up, but now she wears it all the time.*
>
> TIP

Grammar in action

④ We use **used to** for past habits and situations when we want to emphasize that things are different now:

> *I used to believe in love at first sight. Now I'm more cynical.*

⑤ We use the **past simple**, not **used to**, with exact dates, times, numbers of times, and periods of time:

> *My dad went on business trips to Japan four times last year.* (NOT ~~used to go~~)
> *This building was a cinema from 1940 to 1992.* (NOT ~~used to be~~)

But we can use either the **past simple** or **used to** when we don't give an exact time reference:

> *I went / used to go on lots of business trips when I was younger.*
> *The tall building was / used to be a fire station at one point.*

⑥ We can use the **past continuous** or the **past simple** to give background information, and **used to** to explain a habit or situation:

> *When we lived here, there didn't use to be a swimming pool.*
> *When I was learning Spanish, I used to memorize ten words a day.*

C   How things change

For these people, write in an expression with *used to* in order to contrast the present situation with the earlier situation.

0 Eric doesn't smoke nowadays but he <u>used to smoke</u> 40 a day when he was younger.

0 Penny and Sam <u>didn't use to listen</u> to classical music at all but they listen to it all the time now.

1 There .... some old houses here but, as you can see, now there's a supermarket.

2 Now Joe goes to bed early but he .... to bed early before he got this job.

3 Zoë has a car now but she .... one when she was at university.

4 Simon .... with his brother but now he lives on his own.

5 Carol goes to work by bike now but she .... by car.

6 Sandra .... coffee but now she drinks three or four cups a day.

D In the past

Tick the verb phrases that are correct and rewrite the incorrect ones, using *used to* where possible.

0 The lights <u>went</u> out while I was getting the lunch ready. yesterday.   ✓

0 When Jim was younger, he <u>wasn't taking</u> much exercise.   *didn't use to take*

1 Three years ago, Tony <u>used to be</u> in the army. ....

2 Sally made several mistakes because she <u>wasn't concentrating</u>. ....

3 I took my umbrella because I could see that it <u>rained</u>. ....

4 When Jill was young, she <u>was keeping</u> a diary. ....

5 The doctor <u>called</u> to see my mother every day last week. ....

6 I read the text again because I <u>wasn't understanding</u> it very well. ....

E Junior tennis champions

Some years ago, Pam and Carl were junior tennis champions. Now they have three young children and don't have much time for tennis. They are being interviewed on television. Write in the correct past form of the verbs in brackets; use *used to* where possible.

TV   How ...*did you get*...⁰ (you, get) to know each other?

PAM   Well, when I was in my early teens I ....¹ (play) tennis two or three times a week and when I ....² (not, play), I ....³ (watch) matches on TV. One day, while I ....⁴ (watch) a boys' match, I ....⁵ (notice) this handsome young player who ....⁶ (wear) earrings. In those days, in general, boys ....⁷ (not, wear) jewellery, and I ....⁸ (think) it was a bit strange. Anyway, he ....⁹ (win) the match and I ....¹⁰ (decide) to send him a fan letter.

TV   So you ....¹¹ (knew) the name of the handsome young player. What ....¹² (happen) next, Carl?

CARL   One day, a letter ....¹³ (arrive) from this fan called Pamela. In those days, I ....¹⁴ (get) a lot of fan mail, but the letter ....¹⁵ (have) a photo. The girl ....¹⁶ (look) very nice and she ....¹⁷ (hold) a tennis racket.

TV   So you ....¹⁸ (arrange) to meet her.

CARL   Yes, but soon we ....¹⁹ (not, have) to arrange to meet because Pam ....²⁰ (start) playing for the young women's team.

TV   You both ....²¹ (become) junior champions, but you don't play any longer.

PAM   No, we ....²² (stop) playing regularly when I ....²³ (expect) Sally, our first daughter.

TV   And do you miss top-class tennis?

CARL   Not really. We ....²⁴ (love) tennis while we ....²⁵ (play) but now we're happy to spend our time with the children.

OVER TO YOU   Now go to page 122.

03 Present perfect
Forms, uses, and contexts; time phrases

1 We form the **present perfect** with **have/has + past participle**:

*Sam **has passed** her exam. (OR Sam**'s passed**…)*
***Has** anyone **seen** my red jacket?*
*They **haven't spoken** to each other for ages.*

(For rules on forming the past participle, and irregular verbs, see p. 129.)

2 We use the **present perfect** to talk about past actions and situations that have a result in the present:

*Alan **has made** a cake. (= There is a cake that we can eat now.)*
***Have** you **tidied** your room? (= Is it tidy now?)*

3 We use the **present perfect** in positive statements with **just** and **already** in the pattern **have/has + just/already + past participle**. **Just** means 'very recently'; **already** means 'before now':

*I**'ve just spoken** to Peter. I phoned him 5 minutes ago.*
*You**'ve already seen** Jaws, so let's see something else.*

4 We use the **present perfect** with **yet** in negatives and questions. **Yet** comes after the past participle, and means 'before/until now':

***Has** the bus **arrived** yet?*
*I **haven't done** my homework **yet**.*

5 We can use **still** before the **negative present perfect** with the meaning 'even now':

*I **still haven't finished** my homework.*

Grammar in action

1 We use the **present perfect** to talk about people's lives until now. This use is often accompanied by **always**, **never**, **ever**, and other time expressions:

I've always been a vegetarian; I've never eaten meat.
Have you ever tasted real caviar?

2 We use the **present perfect** to talk or ask about the result of a recent action that is complete. We can use the present perfect with **how much/many**:

Sally has finished the preparations for the party. ~ Great! How many cakes has she made? ~ She's baked four chocolate cakes and she's made some banana ice cream! (We are thinking about the result of the preparations – that there are lots of cakes.)

3 We can use the **present perfect** to talk about the news:

The president has announced major tax increases.

4 We often use the **present perfect** with **already**, **yet**, and **still** to express surprise:

Our bus still hasn't arrived. (= We expected it to arrive before now.)
England have already scored a goal! (= surprisingly early.)
The postman hasn't been yet. (= We expected him before now, he's surprisingly late.)

A   A job interview

Alina is in an interview for a volunteer job at the local dog refuge. Circle the correct words.

BOSS	So, Alina, why do you want to come and work for us?
ALINA	Well, I've *always* / *never* / *ever* ⁰ loved animals.
BOSS	OK, and do you have any experience of dogs, specifically?
ALINA	Yes, we've had dogs at home *in 2003 / all my life / last year* ¹.
BOSS	So have you *never / yet / ever* ² trained them and looked after them?
ALINA	Yes, in fact, I've *still / just / yet* ³ trained a new puppy.
BOSS	And have you *ever / still / always* ⁴ had to deal with problem dogs?
ALINA	No, I've *still / never / yet* ⁵ worked with problem dogs.
BOSS	Hmm, but you've *always / yet / already* ⁶ spent some time here haven't you?
ALINA	Yes, I've helped out with the paperwork in the office *several times / last week / in June* ⁷, but I haven't worked with the animals *yet / ever / already* ⁸.

B Looking back on life

Here a woman writes about her life. Complete the text by using the words in brackets and putting the verb in the present perfect. Use short forms where possible.

I 've seen⁰ good and bad times but on the whole I ....¹ (have) a good life. I ....² (be) married for over 25 years and I ....³ (have) four children and nearly all of them ....⁴ (find) good jobs. My youngest son ....⁵ (still, not, graduate). But my family ....⁶ (not, be) my only interest. My husband ....⁷ (often, work) abroad and I ....⁸ (manage) to visit most of the places where his company ....⁹ (send) him. In fact, I ....¹⁰ (visit) more than twenty countries and I ....¹¹ (spend) several weeks in most of them. In my spare time, I ....¹² (write) guides to three of them and one of them ....¹³ (already, sell) 10,000 copies. The money ....¹⁴ (just, pay) for a new computer. I'm pleased about that because my publisher ....¹⁵ (just, ask) me to write a book about Portugal.

C Preparations for a party

Some students are arranging an end-of-term party. Carrie is checking whether everything is ready. Use the words given, use the present perfect, and put *just, yet, still,* and *already* in the correct places where necessary. Use short forms.

CARRIE   Are we all here? Has everybody arrived yet ⁰ (everybody / arrive / yet)?

JIM   ....¹ (Ruth / phone / just). She has a problem with her motorbike so ....² (she / not / leave / still) her house, but we can start without her because I know what ....³ (she / do).

CARRIE   All right. Jim, what food ....⁴ (you / buy)?

JIM   ....⁵ (I / not / buy / anything / yet), but ....⁶ (I / order / just) cheese, ham, bread and salad vegetables and ....⁷ (I / ask / already) if they can have it ready early on Saturday morning.

CARRIE   Fine. And drinks?

JIM   Pauline's cousin works in a wine shop. ....⁸ (she / get) us a good discount on most things and ....⁹ (she / promise) to deliver everything in good time.

CARRIE   Great! Bobby, ...¹⁰ (you / find) somewhere that will lend us chairs and tables?

BOBBY   Well, ...¹¹ (I / ask) if we can borrow them from the people at the community centre, but they ....¹² (not / phone back / still).

CARRIE   ....¹³ (I / persuade) my brother's band to come and play for us. And ....¹⁴ (I / check / just) the weather on the internet. It's going to be fine on Saturday.

6 We form the **present perfect continuous** with **have/ has been** + *-ing* form:

> *I've **been watching** you.*
> *They **haven't been playing** long.*
> ***Has** he **been travelling** all day?*

7 We use the **present perfect continuous** to talk about actions that started in the past and continue into the present:

> *The earth **has been getting** warmer.*

8 We use the **present perfect continuous** when the emphasis is on the **action** being done. (To talk about the result of the action, use the present perfect – for more information, see p. 10.)

> *Why is the kitchen in a mess? ~ Because Alan**'s been making** a cake.*
> *Emma's tired. She**'s been tidying** her room all morning. (The job is not necessarily finished.)*

Grammar in action

⑤ We use the **present perfect continuous** to talk about an action we started in the past, and are still doing now:

> *I've been working all day and I still haven't finished.*

⑥ We also use the **present perfect continuous** to talk about an action we started in the past that finished a very short time ago:

> *I've been waiting for you to call.*

⑦ We can use the **present perfect continuous** for a series of repeated actions, for example when we try to do something again and again:

> *We've been trying to contact you all day to tell you that you've won a prize.*

⑧ We use the **present perfect continuous** to talk or ask about an action happening over a period of time up to now. We can use **how long** with **for** or **since**:

> *Sally's been cooking all afternoon. She's been preparing for the party since lunchtime. (We are thinking of Sally doing the cooking.)*

We use the **present perfect continuous** to talk about recent repeated actions or for a repeated action that is different from usual. We use time phrases such as **recently**, **lately**, **this week**.

> *My son's been staying up late a lot recently – I'm rather worried.*

⑨ We often use the **present perfect continuous** when a recent action explains why we look or feel a certain way:

> *Jane's tired because she's been painting her room. (The action of painting explains why she is tired.)*

D   Waiting for the stars

A journalist visits a film festival and talks to the fans waiting to see the film stars.

JOURNALIST   Good morning. How long *have you been waiting* ⁰ (you, wait) to see your favourite stars?

FAN   Well, we arrived at about 6 a.m. and it's 10 a.m. now, so we _____ ¹ (wait) for about four hours.

JOURNALIST   And _____ ² (you, stand) here all that time?

FAN   No, a friend and I take it in turns because of the rain.

JOURNALIST   Yes, it's pretty wet. _____ ³ (it, rain) long?

FAN   No, only since about 9 o'clock.

JOURNALIST   And how about you? Are you a great film festival fan?

FAN   Oh, yes. I _____ ⁴ (come) to this one for six years now.

JOURNALIST   Six years? That's as long as I _____ ⁵ (write) articles for my newspaper. I see you've got an autograph book.

FAN Yes, I always bring it with me. I've got more than 200 autographs.

JOURNALIST Whose autograph are you hoping to get today?

FAN Scarlett Johansson's. I .... ⁶ (try) to get it for years but I still haven't managed it.

E Children

Use the verbs in the present perfect continuous to complete the dialogue.

build	do	feed	look	play	worry

JACK AND EVE Hello, Mummy. We're home.

MOTHER Thank goodness. I _have been looking_ ⁰ for you everywhere. What .... ¹ (you)?

EVE We .... ² in the park.

MOTHER But you're all dirty.

JACK Yes, I .... ³ houses with the mud from the pond.

EVE And I .... ⁴ the ducks.

MOTHER And I .... ⁵ about where you were. Well, you can both go and have a good wash!

F More party preparations

Fiona is in charge of a big party but she arrives late, in the middle of the preparations. Complete the dialogue by putting the verbs into the present perfect simple or the present perfect continuous.

FIONA Hello, everybody. I'm sorry I'm late. I _have been trying_ ⁰ (try) to find a DJ but so far I _haven't found_ ⁰ (not, find) one, though one .... ¹ (promise) to phone me later. .... ² (you all, get on) with what we decided?

KATE Well, Tim and I .... ³ (make) sandwiches ever since we arrived. So far, we .... ⁴ (make) about 50.

FIONA Charlie – .... ⁵ (you, manage) to set up the sound system yet?

CHARLIE Well, I .... ⁶ (work) on it all morning but there are a couple of technical problems that I .... ⁷ (not, solve) yet.

FIONA You look very hot, Mike. I suppose that's because you .... ⁸ (move) the chairs and tables.

MIKE That's right. But I've almost finished, and my sister .... ⁹ (wipe) all of them so they are ready for use.

(RING, RING)

FIONA Oh, that's my mobile. Hello … Yes, I .... ¹⁰ (expect) your call … You can? Oh, that's great! … See you about 9 o'clock then. Bye!

FIONA Great news, everybody. That guy I mentioned .... ¹¹ (agree) to be our DJ.

OVER TO YOU Now go to page 122.

1 Compare the use of the **past simple** and **present perfect**:
   Has the contract arrived yet? ~ Yes, it arrived on Tuesday. I've already signed it.

2

We use the **past simple** to talk about something in thepast, and to say **when** something happened.
 	
   They arrived last week. (= at a specific time in the past)
	We use the **present perfect** to talk about something that happened in the past that is relevant now, and when the exact time that it happened is not important.
	
	   They have arrived. (= some time before now)

3

We use the **past simple** with **for** to talk about a situation that started and finished in the past:
 	
   He lived in Wroclaw for two years before that. (= He doesn't live there now.)
	We use the **present perfect** with **for** to talk about an ongoing situation – something that started in the past and continues to the present moment:
	
	   Patrick has lived in Krakow for six years. (= He lives there now.)
	
	We use the **present perfect** with **since** to talk about when the ongoing situation started, followed by a time or an event:
	
	   Patrick has lived in Krakow since 2004. (2004 = past time)
	   Patrick has lived in Krakow since his wedding. (his wedding = past event)

4

We use the **past simple** with finished-time expressions to say when something happened in the past, e.g.: a period of time + **ago**, **yesterday**, **last week**, **in April**, etc., **in 2004**, etc., **when?**, **what time?**
 	
   Patrick moved to Krakow six years ago.
   What did you do yesterday?
   Did you see Brian last week?
We often use **first** or **last** with the past simple:
 	
   Patrick first moved abroad in 1993.
   I last visited him in June.
	We use time phrases that include the present moment with the **present perfect**, e.g.: **today, this week/month/ summer/year**
	
	   What have you done today?
	   Have you seen Brian this week?

Grammar in action

1. We use the **past simple** to talk about finished events in history:
   Hannibal's army crossed the Alps and fought against the Romans.

   We use the **present perfect** to talk about recent events or achievements in the news:
   Scientists have discovered a new kind of bird in Africa.
   Prince William has opened a theatre.

2. We use the **past simple** with a specific time in the past to talk about situations that are no longer true and we use **used to** when we don't talk about a specific time.

   We use the **present perfect** to talk about situations that are true in the present. Here, we are talking about our town:
   There was a cinema here in the 1970s. There used to be a theatre too. The supermarket has been here for several years (and is still here now).

3. We often use the **present perfect** when we first mention a topic, and then use the **past simple** to talk about it. This is common in conversation:
   Have you heard Xinc's new album? ~ Yes, I bought it yesterday. I liked the first track, but I didn't enjoy the rest of it.

   And it is common in newspapers, TV reports, etc.:
   Police have charged a local man with arson. They arrested Joe Dunce last night, questioned him for six hours, and pressed charges this afternoon.

A In New York City

Two colleagues meet by chance on holiday in New York. Complete the conversation by crossing out the form that doesn't fit.

MEL Nell, fancy meeting you here. *Were you / Have you been* [0] here long?

NELL No, we *came / 've come* [1] the day before yesterday.

MEL I don't think you *met / 've met* [2] my partner, Barry.

NELL Yes, we *met / 've met* [3] at the Christmas party.

MEL You're not here on your own, are you?

NELL No, my sister's with me, but she *stayed / 's stayed* [4] in the hotel because she *didn't sleep / hasn't slept* [5] very well since we *got / 've got* [6] here.

MEL We *were / 've been* [7] here for a week and so far we *really enjoyed / 've really enjoyed* [8] it.

NELL I *read / 've read* [9] a couple of books about New York before we *set off / 've set off* [10].

MEL Yes, we *did / have* [11], too. We *ate / 've eaten* [12] at a couple of places that the books *recommended / have recommended* [13]. In fact, we *went / 've been* [14] to a very good restaurant last night.

NELL And *did you visit / have you visited* [15] the Empire State Building yet?

MEL Yes, but there *was / has been* [16] an enormous queue so we *decided / 've decided* [17] to walk up the stairs. I *never climbed / 've never climbed* [18] so many stairs in my life.

B My home town

Two people talk about some changes in the city where they grew up. Complete the conversation with the correct forms of the words in the box and the words in brackets.

agree	become	bring	change	close	get	go	like	live	produce	visit

PAT I __went__ [0] to Sheffield a couple of weeks ago. The city _____ [1] a lot since you and I _____ [2] there. It's a nicer place to live in now.

VAL I _____ [3] (not) the city for a while but I hear that it _____ [4] a lot cleaner.

PAT Yes, in the old days the steelworks _____ [5] a lot of smoke, but most of them _____ [6] now. And you remember that they _____ [7] rid of the trams in the 1950s.

VAL Yes, I _____ [8] (not) with that at the time because I _____ [9] riding on the trams.

PAT Well, guess what! They _____ [10] them back.

VAL That is good news. I can see that I'll have to go back for a visit.

> **WORD FOCUS**
>
> Find a phrase in exercise B that has this meaning:
>
> took away
> ....

5 We form the **past perfect** with **had + past participle**:
*They **had taken** lots of photos.*
*What **had** the boys **done**?*
*She **hadn't finished** her course.*

(For more information on past participles, see p. 129.)

6 When we talk about two things in the past, we use the **past perfect** for the earlier event; this is to make clear which action happened first. Compare:
We forgot to take our umbrellas and we got very wet.
→ *We got very wet because we'd forgotten to take our umbrellas.*

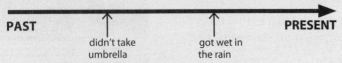

PAST   PRESENT
didn't take umbrella   got wet in the rain

I posted the letter before my wife mentioned it.
→ *When my wife mentioned the letter, I **had** already **posted** it.*

7 We often use the words **although**, **before**, **until**, **already**, and **never** with the **past perfect**:
*I **had never seen** an elephant **until** I went to India.*

8 We use the **past perfect** in indirect speech. We use it to report both the present perfect and the past simple:
*'I **have** never **used** a mobile phone,' said Philip.*
(present perfect) → *Philip told me that he **had** never **used** a mobile phone.*
*'I **passed** my test in September,' Mary told Ben.* (past simple) → *Mary told Ben that she **had passed** her test in September.*

(For more information on indirect speech, see units 13 and 14.)

Grammar in action

4 We use both the **past perfect** and the **past continuous** to give background information.

We use the **past perfect** to say what happened **before** something else happened:
Everyone had arrived when he started his presentation.

We use the **past continuous** to say what happened **around the time** that something else happened:
People were still arriving when he started his presentation.

5 We often use the **past perfect** after verbs of thinking, e.g. **think, know, believe, decide, forget, remember**, to say what we thought at an earlier time:
I thought we had agreed to get the 3.30 train.
Suzy knew we had forgotten her birthday.

6 We **do not use** the **past perfect** when we give a series of actions in the **order they happened**:
We sat down and we ordered our food. Then the fire alarm went off and we left the café.

But we do use the **past perfect** when we report the events in a **different order**:
We ordered our food after we had sat down…

And we can move the details of what we say into the background with the **past perfect**, keeping the most important or interesting information in the past simple:
We had sat down and ordered our food when the fire alarm went off.

C The reason why there was a problem

Complete the explanations by using a verb from the box in the past perfect. Use short forms where possible.

| be | cause | create | do | see | tell |

LAURA   Lucy was expelled from school because she had upset some of the teachers.
JANE   How ___had___ she ___done___ ⁰ that?
LAURA   She .... ¹ a web page criticizing the teachers. Some of the teachers .... ² it and they .... ³ the headmaster, so he expelled her on Monday. It seems a bit unfair, she .... ⁴ a student there for three years when they expelled her, and she .... ⁵ (never) any trouble before that.

apologize	fall	make	notice	put	steal	not take

JAKE   The store detective accused my brother Tim of stealing.

BEN   What .... he .... [6]?

JAKE   Nothing. The detective .... [7] a mistake. He stopped Tim because he thought that Tim .... [8] some books in his bag, but the books .... [9] on the floor and nobody .... [10]. My brother .... [11] anything without paying. Tim was really angry and refused to leave the store until the detective .... [12].

D   A report for the director

When a manager comes back from a business trip, he asks his staff what happened while he was away.

MANAGER   Have there been any major problems while I was away?

ALICE   No, nothing special.

MANAGER   That's good to hear, Alice. And how are those drawings going?

ALICE   Fine, I didn't finish them till last Friday but I sent them to the client on Monday.

MANAGER   Good work. And Phil – have you arranged things with the insurance company?

PHIL   Yes, I received their proposal on Monday and I've already written a reply.

MANAGER   Fine. What about the new photocopier, David?

DAVID   It hasn't arrived yet but I phoned Jacksons on Tuesday to remind them that the agreement was for delivery this week.

With this information, the manager writes a report for the director. Complete it by putting the verbs in brackets into the past perfect. Use long forms.

Yesterday morning I checked what _had happened_ [0] (happen) while I was away. They told me that there .... [1] (be) no major problems. Alice explained that she .... [2] (not finish) the drawings until last Friday but she .... [3] (send) them to the client on Monday. Phil reported that he .... [4] (receive) the insurance proposal on Monday and that he .... already .... [5] (write) a reply. David told me that the new photocopier .... [6] (not arrive) but he .... [7] (phone) Jacksons to remind them that they .... [8] (agree) to deliver it this week. I told you before I went that I .... [9] (leave) instructions for my staff and you can see that they have worked well.

OVER TO YOU   Now go to page 122.

1 We can talk about future actions using the **present tense** of **be** with **going to + verb**. These are the forms:
> *Look at those dark clouds. It's not going to be sunny this weekend, it's going to rain.*
> *I'm going to buy some new shoes tomorrow.*
> *When are you going to speak to your boss?*

2 We use **going to** to talk about something that is about to happen because of a previous decision:
> *We haven't got any sugar. ~ I know. I'm going to buy some this afternoon.* (= she has already decided)

3 We use **going to** to predict future actions and events, when we base our predictions on evidence or knowledge:
> *That pile of boxes doesn't look safe. I think they're going to fall.* (I can see they don't look safe.)
> *This snow is going to ruin my plants.* (I know that snow can do this.)

Grammar in action

1 We can use **going to** to talk about things that we plan to do or things that we have already decided to do:
> *I've got several things to do before I go on holiday. Tomorrow I'm going to have a haircut and buy some new shorts. On Friday I'm going to print out the tickets and check in online. And on Saturday, before I leave, I'm going to put all the pot plants outside so that my neighbour can water them.*

2 We can use **going to** to talk about planned changes:
> *The sports club is going to build a new swimming pool. ~ What are they going to do with the old one? ~ They're going to turn it into two tennis courts.*

3 We can use **going to** to make predictions about future events in our own lives or in the world, especially when we have a reason for our predictions:
> *Because of climate change, this area's going to be desert in a few years' time.*
> *Why do you look so worried? ~ I haven't done any work, so I'm going to fail my exam.*

4 We can use **going to** with '**… or not**' to talk about something that has been planned but which appears not to be happening; the speaker wants to confirm that the action is going to happen:
> *Well, are you going to come with me or not?*

A Plan, change, prediction or confirmation?

Look at these sentences, taken from a newspaper. Which of the usages in *Grammar in action* do they show? Write 1, 2, 3 or 4.

0 The euro is getting stronger and stronger. It's going to be worth as much as the pound soon. [3]

1 The new government has announced that they aren't going to invest in nuclear energy. [ ]

2 There's a sale on tomorrow. I'm going to look for some new garden furniture. [ ]

3 Scientists observing the volcano say that it isn't going to erupt. [ ]

4 'Is the Prime Minister going to apologize or not?' the opposition leader demanded. [ ]

5 'I've just spoken to her', Moss's agent said, 'and she said she's going to stay in Spain for another week.' [ ]

6 The factory is going to move production of all new cars to China next year. [ ]

B The week ahead

Look at Mike's diary. Then complete what he says about his week's plans with the *going to* form of the verbs in the box. Use short forms.

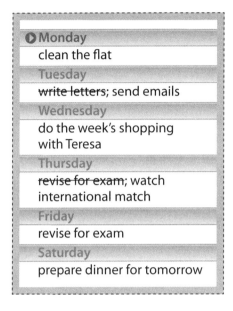

▶ **Monday**
clean the flat
Tuesday
~~write letters~~; send emails
Wednesday
do the week's shopping with Teresa
Thursday
~~revise for exam~~; watch international match
Friday
revise for exam
Saturday
prepare dinner for tomorrow

clean	do	help	prepare	not revise
revise	send	show	watch	not write

This evening, I *'m going to clean* [0] my flat. Tomorrow, I _____ [1] some emails. I have decided I _____ [2] letters because emails are so much quicker. On Wednesday, I _____ [3] the week's shopping. Not on my own this time because Teresa _____ [4] me. On Thursday evening, some friends and I _____ [5] the international match on TV so I _____ [6] for my exam that night. Instead, I _____ [7] for it on Friday. On Saturday, I _____ [8] the dinner for Sunday because my parents are coming on Sunday and I _____ [9] them what a good cook I am now!

C Brisport town council's plans

The Brisport town council wants to attract more tourists. Complete this interview with the mayor using the *going to* form of the verbs. Use long forms.

INTERVIEWER: With the government money you can now go ahead with your plans. Tell us some of the things that you *are you going to do* [0] (do). How _____ you _____ [1] (attract) more tourists?

MAYOR: Well, the Works Department _____ [2] (clean) the Town Hall and the Parks Department _____ [3] (improve) the zoo.

INTERVIEWER: That sounds good. What about cultural attractions?

MAYOR: The Culture Department _____ [4] (renovate) the museum but unfortunately we _____ [5] (not install) an audio guide system. We couldn't get the funding this time.

INTERVIEWER: Hmm. That _____ [6] (disappoint) some people. What about information for the tourists?

MAYOR: Well, we _____ [7] (upgrade) the town website and the Tourist Department _____ [8] (employ) two new guides.

INTERVIEWER: And what about the councillors? _____ they _____ [9] (get) their money, or not?

MAYOR: I'm afraid they _____ [10] (not get) the pay rise they expected.

4 We can talk about the future using **will + verb**:
*I **will be** 40 years old in January.*
***Will** the parcel **arrive** in time?*
*There **will not be** any pay rises this year.*

With **I** and **we** we also use **shall + verb**:
*I **shall be** at home tomorrow.*
*We **shall arrive** early.*

5 We often use the positive short form **'ll** and the negative short form **won't**:
*I**'ll** soon **be** 40 years old but I **won't feel** any older.*

The negative short form of **shall** is **shan't**:
*I **shan't be** much longer.*

6 We use **will** to express certainty and make predictions about the future:
*They **will announce** the results at 9p.m. this evening.*
*The Republicans **will lose**, I think.*

7 We use **will** to make offers and suggestions:
*I**'ll help** you with your homework.*

We also use the question form **Shall I / Shall we … + verb**? to make suggestions and offers:
***Shall** we **go** to the cinema tonight?*
***Shall** I **book** the tickets?*

8 We use **will** to make promises, requests, threats, and warnings:
***Will** you **help** me move house? ~ Yes, of course I **will**.*
*Stop talking, or I**'ll send** you outside the classroom.*

9 **Will** is sometimes used to express 'willingness', i.e. a desire to do something:
*I know you like swimming. **Will** you **teach** her, as I haven't got time any more?* (= Are you happy to teach her?)

Grammar in action

⑤ We can use **will/shall** to give a view of how the world might be in a few years' time, or to make predictions about our lives:
*We certainly **won't travel** as much as we do now because aeroplane fuel will be so expensive.*
What will my life be like in 10 years' time? I imagine I'll be married or at least I'll have a steady partner. I'm not sure whether we'll have any children.

⑥ We use **will/shall** in positive sentences and **shall** in questions to make offers and suggestions, for example offering to help someone:
Shall I help you with your suitcase?
I'll give you a lift to the airport.

⑦ When we make a spontaneous decision at the moment of speaking, we use **will/shall**:
We haven't got any sugar. ~ Really? OK, I'll buy some this afternoon.

⑧ We use **will** in question forms to make informal requests:
Will you give me a hand, please? (= Will you help me?)

D The optimist and the pessimist

Complete the opinions of the optimist and pessimist with *will* or *won't*. Circle the correct word.

OPTIMIST   In a few years, medical science (will)/ won't ⁰ eliminate most diseases.

PESSIMIST No, rich people *will / won't*¹ have access to doctors but poor people *will / won't*² and they *will / won't*³ continue to suffer.

OPTIMIST   Farmers *will / won't*⁴ produce enough food for everybody so there *will / won't*⁵ be any hungry people.

PESSIMIST Food *will / won't*⁶ become more and more expensive and poor countries *will / won't*⁷ be able to buy it.

OPTIMIST   Scientists *will / won't*⁸ find ways to produce cheap energy and the world *will / won't*⁹ be much cleaner.

PESSIMIST   Perhaps there *will/won't* [10] be cheap energy for some people but there *will/won't* [11] be enough for everybody.

OPTIMIST   Wars *will/won't* [12] no longer exist and people *will/won't* [13] live together in harmony.

PESSIMIST   Maybe there *will/won't* [14] be any traditional wars, but people *will/won't* [15] fight for water and other basic resources.

E   A family argument

Sophia and her parents are having an argument. Complete the conversation with *will*, *won't* or *shall*.

MUM   Sophia is still in her room. She __won't__ [0] come down. _____ [1] you talk to her or _____ [2] I?

DAD   _____ [3] we do it together?

MUM   OK. Sophia, _____ [4] you come out and discuss this like an adult, please?

SOPHIA   I _____ [5] only discuss it like an adult if you treat me like an adult.

DAD   Sophia, I _____ [6] put up with this much longer.

SOPHIA   Then I _____ [7] stay in my room.

MUM   Look, come out, and I promise we _____ [8] listen to your points.

SOPHIA   But you still _____ [9] let me go out clubbing, will you?

DAD   Wendy, this isn't working, is it? _____ [10] we give up for now?

WORD FOCUS

Find a phrase in exercise E that has this meaning:

tolerate

_____

F   Talking about the future

Complete these sentences using *will* or *going to* and explain your answers using the phrases from the box.

> offer   spontaneous decision   warning   promise
> prediction based on evidence   decision made in advance

0   You're so sunburned! That __'s going to hurt__ (hurt) tomorrow!
__prediction based on evidence__

1   Don't steal those apples! I _____ (call) the police!
_____

2   Is that suitcase heavy? I _____ (help) you carry it upstairs.
_____

3   Look! There's Kelly. I _____ (go) and say hello to her quickly.
_____

4   I booked our holiday yesterday. We _____ (drive) across America in a vintage Cadillac! _____

5   I'm sorry I broke your vase. I _____ (buy) you a new one tomorrow. _____

OVER TO YOU   Now go to page 122.

1 We use **can, could, be able to**, and **managed to** like this:

> He **can** | VERB cook.
> He **could** | cook.

> She **was able to** | VERB finish | on time.
> She **managed to** | finish | on time.

2 **Can** and **could** always have the same form.
> Timmy **can play** the piano.
> When I was 7, I **could swim** more than 200 metres.

The negative forms are **cannot** (one word) and **could not** (two words), with short forms **can't** and **couldn't**.
> We **cannot accept** applications after the closing date.
> She's sorry she **couldn't come** yesterday.

We start questions with **can** and **could** (not *do*).
> **Can** you **speak** another language?
> (NOT ~~Do you can speak…~~)
> **Could** you **ride** a bike when you were four?
> (NOT ~~Did you could ride…~~)

3 Ability
We use **can** to talk about ability:
> Our daughter **can tie** her own shoes.
> How many languages **can** you **speak**?

4 We use **could** to talk about past ability in general:
> Sam **couldn't walk** until he was 18 months old.
> **Could** you **write** before you started school?

5 We usually express future ability with **will be able to**:
> You'**ll be able to operate** the machinery at the end of this course.

But we can use **can** if the ability to do something in the future depends on something else happening in the present or future:
> You **can** / **will be able to pass** this exam if you start revising now.

6 We use **was/were able to** and **managed to** for actions that were completed at a particular moment in the past:
> The coach caught fire but all the passengers **were able** / **managed to escape**.

Grammar in action

1 We use **can** and **could** to talk about ability, for example when we describe skills in work or education:
> We need someone who can work well in teams and on their own, and can use PCs and Macs.
> Last year, Paul could only say a few words of English but now he can say whole sentences.

2 We use **could** to talk about general skills in the past. This might be a skill in sport:

> I could run a marathon in under three hours when I was younger.

But we use **was able to** or **managed to** to talk about our ability to do something specific at a certain time in the past – for example, one particular achievement:
> Because I trained for six months, I managed to run the 2009 London Marathon in under 3 hours.

3 We often use **can** instead of the present simple to talk about the senses (with **see, hear, feel, taste**, and **smell**):
> I've got a cold, so I can't smell the coffee.
> (NOT NORMALLY I don't smell …)
> I can see the waiter walking this way.
> (NOT NORMALLY I see the waiter …)
> Can you taste the lemon in this cake?
> (NOT NORMALLY Do you taste …)

> We often use **managed to** to express our ability to do something difficult:
> > The piano was heavy but I managed to move it by myself.
>
> TIP

A Modern technology

Complete this text about modern technology with *can, can't, could* or *couldn't*.

You __can't__ ⁰ deny that modern technology has changed our lives. With it, we
__can__ ⁰ do things now that we .... ¹ do at all only a few years ago.
For example, 10 years ago you .... ² only phone from a building or
a telephone box but now we .... ³ make a call wherever we are, and
previously you .... ⁴ only use telephones to make phone calls but now
you .... ⁵ also take photos with them. Of course, in the old days you
.... ⁶ take photos with a camera, but you .... ⁷ take them
without a film. Digital cameras .... ⁸ take hundreds of photos without a
film, though you still .... ⁹ make copies of your photos without a printer.

Another thing is music. A few years ago you .... ¹⁰ only listen to your
music collection at home but now, thanks to MP3 players, you .... ¹¹
listen to it in the street or on the bus.

As for computers, 20 years ago people .... ¹² do simple sums with
a calculator but today, modern computers .... ¹³ solve enormous
mathematical problems in a few seconds. And then there's the Internet. With the Internet
you .... ¹⁴ send messages in an instant, and if you've got a question,
you .... ¹⁵ use Wikipedia to find the answer. My grandfather says that he
.... ¹⁶ believe how quickly everything has changed, he's always saying
that you .... ¹⁷ do any of those things when he was young. However, as I
tell him, you .... ¹⁸ enjoy the benefits of mobile phones, digital cameras,
and computers unless you have enough money to pay for them.

WORD FOCUS

Find words in exercise A that have these meanings:

A in the past

....

B very big

....

C advantages

....

B Generation differences

Complete this text by putting in each of the expressions in the blanks.

be able	can	can't	can't	could	could
couldn't	managed	will be able	were able		

When my father was young, he didn't have much money so he __could__ ⁰
hardly afford any luxuries. I .... ¹ remember exactly when he
met my mother, but it was love at first sight. They worked in the same factory
but they .... ² see each other during the week because they
worked different shifts. One day my mother said, "We .... ³
be young lovers for ever. If we don't save some money, I don't know when
we'll .... ⁴ to get married." My father .... ⁵
see that she was right: they had to do something. So he started working an
extra shift at the weekend and my mother started to take evening classes
to learn accountancy. She didn't have much time to study but at the end
of the year she .... ⁶ to pass the exam and get a job in the
accounts department, which was better paid. After another six months they
had enough savings and they .... ⁷ to get a flat of their own.
Things are easier for my generation. My sister and I .... ⁸ buy
almost anything we want. I hope my children .... ⁹ to say the
same.

7 We use **can, could, may** and **would** like this:

May I | **VERB come** | *in?*

The short form of **would** is **'d**.

8 Permission

We use **can** to give and refuse permission in the present:

> *You **can go** to the party, but you **can't stay** later than 10 o' clock.*

For permission in general in the past we use **could** or **was/were allowed to**:

> *She was spoilt as a child – she **could do** anything she wanted.*

But to talk about permission at a specific time in the past, we must use **was/were allowed to**:

> *I **was allowed to go** to the party last Friday, but I **wasn't allowed to stay** later than 10 o'clock.*

9 We use **can, could** and **may** to ask for permission to do something. We usually use **may** only with **I** or **we** in questions:

> ***Can** we **stop** and have a rest now, please?*
> ***Could** we **finish** early this Friday, please?*
> ***May** I **take** this book home?*

10 Requests

We use **can, could, will** and **would** when we ask someone to do something. **Would** is more polite:

> ***Can** you **explain** this to me?*
> ***Will** you **lend** me your dictionary?*
> ***Would** you **pass** that book, please?*

Grammar in action

4 We use **can** and **will** for permission and requests in informal situations, such as when we're having a meal with family or friends:

> *Will you carve the meat, please?*
> *Can I have some more carrots, please?*

5 We use **could, may** and **would** in more formal situations, such as when talking to a teacher or senior colleague:

> *Would you sign this form, please?*
> *Please could I leave the lesson five minutes early?*

6 We use **could** to talk about things that we had permission to do in the past when the suggestion is 'for the whole of my childhood', 'throughout the 80s and 90s', etc.:

> *We could play out in the streets after dark as children, but I wouldn't let my sons do that.*

When we are talking about having permission to do something on one specific occasion, we use **was/were allowed to**:

> *There was one time I was allowed to miss school for a football match, but usually my parents were too strict.*

C How to be polite

Make these requests polite by using the modal in brackets, *you*, and *please*.

0 Tell Mrs Clarke that I've arrived. (would)

> Would you tell Mrs Clarke that I've arrived, please?

1 Invite Mr Jones for an interview. (can)

2 Take a message. (could)

3 Ask Jim to email me. (would)

4 Collect the report from reception. (would)

D The surprise party

Complete this email using the phrases from the box.

> be able   can   can do   could   could organize   Could you   couldn't
> I'll be able   managed to   managed to book   we can   weren't allowed
> you help   you'll be able to help

Hi Olivia,

I'm trying to organize a surprise party for my sister, but I don't think I _can do_ ⁰ everything myself. When I was a student I _____ ¹ huge events for my rowing club all by myself, but I must be out of practice! _____ ² help me, please? Last week, I _____ ³ the community centre for the party, but I _____ ⁴ find anyone to help with the food. _____ ⁵ to make a birthday cake on the day, but _____ ⁶ you buy some drinks and crisps?

I've booked the centre until midnight and we _____ ⁷ stay until 12.30 – that half an hour will be our cleaning-up time! At a party I went to last year, we _____ ⁸ to play any music after 11.00 because of the neighbours! We'll _____ ⁹ to have a proper party this time, though, as the community centre's in the middle of a sports field, so no one will hear us!

Anyway, could _____ ¹⁰ me for an hour or so before the party so _____ ¹¹ get everything ready? The DJ is booked and I've invited everyone already. Sophie keeps her address book with her all the time, but I _____ ¹² print out her email address book on Friday.

I think that's everything! I hope _____ ¹³!

Sarah

E A young worker talks to his boss

Cross out the incorrect options.

WORKER I *would like / want* ⁰ to speak to you for a moment. *May / Do* I ¹ come in?

BOSS I *can't / may not* ² see you at the moment because I'm busy. *Can / May* ³ you come at about 10 o'clock?

(*Later*)

WORKER *Could / Would* ⁴ I have a word with you now?

BOSS Yes, come in. What *can / may* ⁵ I do for you?

WORKER Well, today is my mother's birthday. Yesterday I finished work late. I *could / managed to* ⁶ buy her a birthday card from the stationer's, but the big shops were closed so I *can't / couldn't* ⁷ get her a present.

BOSS So you *want / would* ⁸ to finish work early today so you *can / may* ⁹ buy her a present. Is that it?

WORKER Yes, that's it exactly.

BOSS All right. But remember you won't *be able to / can* ¹⁰ use the same excuse until next year!

OVER TO YOU Now go to page 123.

1 We use **must, can't, may, might** and **could** like this:

Jenny *might* │VERB know│ *the answer,*

2 Certainty

We use **must** to say that we are certain:

*I haven't seen the neighbours all week. They **must be** away.* (= From what I know, I can be certain that the neighbours are away.)

*Lara has her hair done almost every day. It **must cost** a fortune.* (= I can be certain that it costs a lot of money.)

3 Impossibility

We use **can't** to say that something is impossible:

*The man in the photo **can't be** Peter because he never wears a hat.* (= From what we know, we can say that the man is **not** Peter.)

*Anna **can't win** the race now - she's too far behind.* (= We can predict that Anna **won't** win the race.)

4 Possibility

We use **may, might** and **could** to talk about present possibilities, and to talk about future possibilities:

*Your blue shirt **may be** in the big cupboard.* (= From what we know, **perhaps** the shirt **is** in the cupboard.)

*She **might come** and see you tomorrow.* (= From what we know, **perhaps** she **will** come.)

We use **may not** and **might not** (**mightn't**) in negative sentences, but not **could not**. We use these structures to say that it is possible that something won't happen:

*Ed **may not know** how to find our house.* (OR *Ed **might not know** ...*) (= **Perhaps** he **won't** know ...)

Grammar in action

1 We use **must** and **can't** to draw definite conclusions about present situations based on what we know:

*I can hear sounds from that room. There **must be** someone in there.*

*The rooms at that hotel are quite cheap. The price **can't include** breakfast.*

2 We can use **may, might** and **could** to explore options for the future, for example when discussing a possible career:

*I don't know yet what I'm going to do after I finish. I **may stay** on at university or I **could take** a year off and go abroad. Someone **might offer** me a job!*

3 We can use **may, might** or **could** to help make suggestions in order to solve a problem:

*Do you know where the camera is? ~ I'm not sure. It **might be** in one of the desk drawers or it **may be** in the cupboard.*

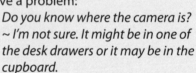

4 We use **may, might** and **could** to guess about a situation in the present when we don't know all the facts:

*Where's Mike? ~ There **might be** a problem with his train. ~ Yes, or he **could be** at the café already.*

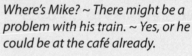

A Choosing a present

Complete this conversation with *must* or *can't* and one of the verbs from the box.

| be | be | cost | have | love | mean | think |

ANDY   I need some money. There must be⁰ a bank round here somewhere.

MAX   Yes, round that corner, I think. What do you want the money for?

ANDY   To buy one of those new mobile phones for Kate.

MAX   They ....¹ a fortune! I've never bought Maria anything like that.

ANDY   Well, you ....² her very much then.

MAX   You ....³ that money can buy people.

ANDY   Well, it can!

MAX   You ....⁴ that seriously.

ANDY   No, not really. But Kate's very attractive. She ....⁵ plenty of admirers and I don't want to lose her.

MAX   But you told me that she wanted to marry you so she 6
         interested in other men.

ANDY   That's true. Perhaps I should buy her a ring instead and make it definite.

B   But have you thought about …?

In these short dialogues, the second person mentions something that the first
person has not considered. Use *may* or *may not* and one of the verbs from the box to
complete the sentences.

> be   come   decide   get   have   like   prefer   want

KIM   We're going to give our visitors fish for lunch.

SAM   They ___*may not like*___ 0 fish. They ___*may prefer*___ 0 meat.

RUTH   Our plan is to take our guests for a long walk as soon as they get here.

BEN   They .... 1 to rest after their journey. In any case, they
         .... 2 walking shoes with them.

LEO   I'm going to ask my uncle to give me a ride on his motorbike.

ANNE   He .... 3 on his motorbike. He .... 4 to come by car.

LUKE   I'm going to wait for our guests to arrive.

NAOMI   They .... 5 here until this afternoon. There 6
         a lot of traffic today.

WORD FOCUS

Find a word in
exercise C that
means 'some
money from the
government to pay
for their education'.

....

C   What to do, where to go

Holly and Adam have just got married and have gone on their honeymoon. A friend
talks to Holly's mother about their plans for the future. Rewrite the parts in brackets
using *must*, *can't* or *may/might*.

FRIEND   Just married and on their honeymoon. ___They must be___ 0 (I'm sure they're)
         very happy. Where are they going to live after they come back?

MOTHER   ___They may stay___ 0 (Perhaps they'll stay) with us for a while.

FRIEND   What about work?

MOTHER   They .... 1 (Maybe they'll go) abroad for a year.

FRIEND   So Holly .... 2 (I assume that Holly's not) very interested in the
         job she's got. I thought she enjoyed her work.

MOTHER   She does, but they both have one of those temporary contracts, and the
         company .... 3 (perhaps the company won't renew) them.

FRIEND   Yes, that's always a possibility.

MOTHER   Or they .... 4 (maybe they'll take) a postgraduate course.

FRIEND   Would they get a grant?

MOTHER   No, I don't think so but they've both worked for a couple of years so they
         .... 5 (I'm sure they have) some savings.

FRIEND   But Adam's father has his own business, doesn't he? He 6
         (Maybe he'll find) work for them.

MOTHER   I'm not sure. Holly quite likes Adam's father but she 7
         (perhaps she won't want) to work for him.

FRIEND   You see. It's not easy to work for in-laws and it .... 8 (I'm sure it
         isn't) easy to live with them, either.

MOTHER   All right. I see your point.

5 We use **must** and **can't/couldn't** + **have** + **past participle** when we are certain about situations in the past. **Must** and **can't** are opposites:

*I can't find my keys. I **must have left** them at home.* (= I realize it is true that I left my keys at home.)
*I couldn't open the garage door. ~ You **can't have tried** very hard; it wasn't locked.* (= I realize it is impossible that you tried very hard.)

6 We use **may/might/could** + **have** + **past participle** to talk about possibilities in past time:

*Sally said she would call round this morning but she hasn't come. ~ She **may/might/could have** called while we were at the shops.* (= Perhaps she called then.)
*I'm not sure what sort of bird it was that I saw, but it **may/might/could have been** an eagle.* (= Perhaps it was an eagle.)

Grammar in action

⑤ We can use **must** and **can't** + **have** + **past participle** to draw definite conclusions based on evidence. Here, we are talking about a crime investigation:

The thieves stole a very heavy chest. It must have weighed a hundred kilos. One man alone can't have moved it so there must have been two or three of them.

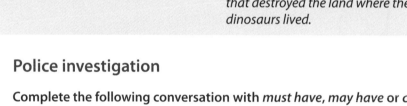

⑥ We can use **may/might/could** + **have** + **past participle** to guess about the possible causes of things in the past:

We're not sure why the dinosaurs died out. An asteroid might have hit the earth, causing a dust storm that blocked out the sun and this could have led to a serious shortage of food. On the other hand, there may have been geological changes that destroyed the land where the dinosaurs lived.

D Police investigation

Complete the following conversation with *must have*, *may have* or *can't have* and the correct form of the verb in brackets.

INSPECTOR What do we know about the body that was found in the river?

CONSTABLE It was of a fairly young man. He _must have been_[0] (be) in his twenties. Judging by his appearance, he ....[1] (be) older than 30 or so. There were no marks on the body so he ....[2] (die) of natural causes, but we can't be sure, so we're treating it as a murder case.

INSPECTOR What else do we know?

CONSTABLE If someone drowns, they have water in their lungs, as you know. In this case, there was no water in the man's lungs, so he ....[3] (drown). He ....[4] (die) before falling into the water.

INSPECTOR Go on.

CONSTABLE There was food in his stomach, so he ....[5] (have) something to eat not long before he died. There ....[6] (be) poison in the food, of course, but we won't know that until we get the chemical analysis. And another thing, his wallet was in his jacket and there was quite a lot of money in it. So if he was murdered, the murderer ....[7] (kill) him for his money.

INSPECTOR Didn't his wallet have any identification?

CONSTABLE No, but there was a recent prescription for sleeping pills so he ....[8] (see) a doctor not so long ago.

INSPECTOR Has anyone reported a missing person matching his description?

CONSTABLE No, so I'm sure he .... [9] (have) any family or friends round here. He .... [10] (be) a stranger to this part of the country.

INSPECTOR Well, put all this in a report and let me know when you find anything else.

E Portrait of a genius

Complete this text about Leonardo da Vinci with *must have*, *might have* or *can't have* and the correct form of one of the words in brackets.

| be be have imagine invent learn meet pose recognize |

Leonardo da Vinci (1452-1519) was a genius as a painter, sculptor and engineer.

People _must have recognized_ [0] his talent early because he worked with the painter Verrocchio from the age of 14. Everyone in Verrocchio's studio had to work together on a variety of projects, so this is where Leonardo .... [1] about metal and wood as well as painting materials. He .... [2] for Verrocchio's statue of David but there is no evidence for this.

There is no record for Leonardo between 1476 and 1481. He .... [3] his own workshop at this time, but we can't be sure.

In 1495 Leonardo paid for the funeral of a woman called Caterina. At first people thought that Caterina was a servant girl, but she .... [4] simply a servant because the funeral was expensive. Nowadays, historians believe that Caterina .... [5] Leonardo's mother, but the evidence is not definite.

Leonardo .... [6] his great contemporary Michelangelo in about 1503, because the two of them worked together for the government in Florence.

Leonardo drew helicopters, tanks and submarines. He was aware that technology was not yet advanced enough for them to be made, but he .... [7] that centuries would pass before they became reality.

There is a legend that King François of France held Leonardo as he was dying. This is possible but not very likely. Some people believe that later painters .... [8] this detail in order to have a famous subject that they could paint, but not everybody agrees.

OVER TO YOU Now go to page 123.

08 Duty and obligation
Should, ought to, have (got) to

1 We use **should** and **ought to** like this:

> I **should** | VERB ask.
> They **ought to** | report | it.

2 The negative forms are **should not** and **ought not to**, with short forms **shouldn't** and **oughtn't to**:

> She **oughtn't to mention** the meeting to anybody. It's confidential.
> They **shouldn't let** their children watch those violent films. They're much too young.

3 We use **should** and **ought to** to express an opinion, give advice, or talk about the correct thing to do (someone's duty):

> Have you got a headache? You **should take** an aspirin. (= I think the best thing to do is to take an aspirin.)
> It's illegal and dangerous. They **ought to report** it to the police. (= It is their duty to report it.)

Should and **ought to** mean the same but we use **should** more than **ought to**.

4 We use **should** in questions to ask for advice. **Ought to** is less common in questions:

> What **should** I do about the broken window?

5 We use **have to** like this:

> You **have to** | VERB return | this book before Friday.

We use **have to** to talk about obligation (actions that are necessary because we think they are important, or because there are rules).
We use **do** in negatives, questions and short answers:

> British people **don't have to carry** identity cards. (= They are not obliged to carry them.)
> **Do** we **have to pay** in advance? ~ Yes, you **do**.

6 In informal situations we can express the same meanings with **have got to**; here, we use **have** in negatives, questions and short answers:

> I**'ve got to phone** my mum today.
> I **have**n't **got to get** up early tomorrow. (= I'm not obliged to get up early.)
> **Have** we **got to come** with you? ~ Yes, you **have**.

(Compare **must not** on p. 32 with the use of **don't have to** here.)

> **TIP**
> The meaning of **have (got) to** is stronger than that of **should** or **ought**. Compare:
> I think all schoolchildren **should** wear a uniform. (My opinion; NOT ~~have to.~~)
> When you are on the premises, you really **ought to** wear your uniform. (An expectation, not a strict rule; NOT ~~have to~~)
> At High Storrs School, everybody **has to** wear a uniform. (A school rule; NOT ~~should.~~)

Grammar in action

1 We can use **should** and **ought to** to say what we think is the best course of action, for example when we give advice on how to solve a problem:

> If you have a high temperature, you shouldn't go to work, but you ought to ring and tell them. ~ Should I stay in bed? ~ Perhaps that's the best place to be, and you should drink lots of water or fruit juice.

2 We can also use **should** and **ought to** to say that we think something is someone's duty:

> You ought to thank your grandparents for the present. You should send them a letter or card.

3 We can use **have to** to talk about official procedures and rules:

> What do I have to do to get a passport? ~ You have to fill in an application form and include two photos. ~ Do I have to pay anything? ~ Yes, they cost about £75, I think.

A First job interview

Sheila is going for her first job interview tomorrow. Her mother gives her some advice. Complete the dialogue by writing *should* or *shouldn't* and one of the verbs from the box.

> behave   choose   dress   leave   look   show   wash   wear

MOTHER   If the interview's at 10 a.m., you ___should leave___ [0] by about 9 a.m.
SHEILA   OK. And how _____ I _____ [1]?

MOTHER	Well, you _____² jeans for a start. I think you _____³ something simple but smart, like your blue suit. And I think you _____⁴ your hair before you go.
SHEILA	How _____ I _____⁵ in the interview itself?
MOTHER	Well, you _____⁶ down at the floor all the time. Instead, you _____⁷ interest by always looking at the person who is interviewing you.

B Advice for tourists visiting a foreign country

Complete this advice for tourists by choosing the correct option.

- You *should / have to*⁰ learn a few phrases in the language. Local people like that.
- You *shouldn't / should*¹ always keep your money in a safe place; you *shouldn't / don't have to*² carry it in your back pocket.
- You *ought to / shouldn't*³ leave the main tourist areas; some districts can be dangerous.
- You *ought not to / don't have to*⁴ sunbathe much in the first few days, and you *have to / should*⁵ always use high-factor sun cream.
- You *ought to / ought not to*⁶ avoid drinking tap water and eating unwashed fruit if you are in a remote area. You *ought not to / don't have to*⁷ drink bottled water everywhere, but you *should / shouldn't*⁸ find out if the tap water is safe to drink.
- You *should / shouldn't*⁹ respect local customs and you *shouldn't / don't have to*¹⁰ visit holy places unless you are respectably dressed.
- Make sure you know the local laws. For example, in some countries you *have to / shouldn't*¹¹ carry your passport and driving licence with you when you are driving.

C Joining a hockey club

Petra has decided to join a hockey club so she goes to talk to the trainer. Complete the conversation with *should, shouldn't,* or *(not) have to.*

TRAINER	Hello, Petra. So you want to join the hockey club.
PETRA	Yes, what _do I have to_⁰ (I) do to join?
TRAINER	Well, you _____¹ tell reception your name and phone number. Otherwise we can't contact you.
PETRA	And _____² (I) pay anything?
TRAINER	No, not at first because it's a trial period, so you _____³ pay anything for the first month, but you _____⁴ attend all the practices and matches. That's the rule.
PETRA	And what do you think I _____⁵ wear?
TRAINER	Well, members have no choice: they _____⁶ wear the team colours. But for the trial period you _____⁷ wear good trainers, a T-shirt and shorts.
PETRA	Anything else?
TRAINER	Yes, you _____⁸ eat a lot just before a practice because it might give you indigestion, but you _____⁹ bring a bottle of water with you because hockey is thirsty work.

7 We use **must + verb** when we think it is important to do an action (obligation) and **must not + verb** (**mustn't**) when something is against the rules (prohibition):

> You **must do** exactly what the doctor says.
> You **mustn't take** any photos in here.

We can use **must** in questions, but we normally prefer **have to**:

> Do we **have to stay** until the end of the meeting.
> (less usual = *Must* we **stay** until the end of the meeting?)

8 We use **need to + verb** to talk about an action that we think or feel is necessary:

> You **need to stop** wasting so much time.

We use **do** in negatives, questions and short answers:

> You **don't need to keep** telling me that!
> Do you **need to see** my passport? ~ Yes, I **do**.

We can also use **needn't** in negative sentences:

> You **needn't keep** telling me that!

9 We use **don't have to, don't need to** or **needn't** when something is unnecessary, not **mustn't**:

> You **don't have to / needn't take** your shoes off inside, but you can if you want to. (= It is unnecessary to take your shoes off.)
> Compare: You **mustn't take** your shoes off. (= It is wrong to take your shoes off.)

TIP

Must and **have (got) to** have very similar meanings, but **must** tends to be more personal while **have (got) to** tends to be more impersonal:

> You **must** come to the party. (I'm telling you.)
> You **have to** pass two tests to get a licence. (That's the law.)

Grammar in action

4 We can use **must** and **have to** to tell someone about rules and formalities:

> In Britain you have to drive on the left and everybody has to wear their seat belt all the time. You don't have to pay anything to drive on the motorway but you must drive within the speed limit.

5 We can use **need to** to talk about what is necessary in order to do a job:

> What do we need to do before we start painting? ~ First, we need to move the chairs into the hall. Then we need to cover the table and the cupboards.

6 We use **mustn't** to say that something is wrong, and **don't have to** to say that something is allowed, but not obligatory. This might be when explaining the policies of an institution:

> In my job, you don't have to wear a tie every day, but you mustn't wear jeans.

D   Instructions for Lily

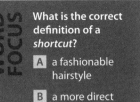

What is the correct definition of a *shortcut*?

A a fashionable hairstyle

B a more direct route

Complete the dialogue with *must, mustn't* or *don't have to*.

MUM   This morning you _must_ ⁰ go and see Grandma.

LILY   Can I go on my bike?

MUM   No, you _____¹ go on your bike because there are some eggs to take.

LILY   What else do I have to take?

MUM   Don't worry. You _____² carry anything else. But it's quite cold so you _____³ wear your warm coat, the red one with the hood.

LILY   Is it all right if I take a shortcut through the wood?

MUM   No, you _____⁴ go through the wood. You _____⁵ stay on the footpath.

LILY   Oh, all right.

MUM	And you _____ [6] get to Grandma's by 11 o'clock because she needs the eggs. So you _____ [7] stop to pick flowers or anything. And above all you _____ [8] talk to any strangers.
LILY	I hope I _____ [9] have lunch at Grandma's. She doesn't cook as well as you do.
MUM	No, you can come home for lunch, but you _____ [10] say anything to Grandma about her cooking.

E   School open day

The local school is having an open day for parents next Saturday. A committee of two teachers and two pupils meets to make arrangements. Complete the discussion with a present simple form of *need* and *to* where necessary.

TEACHER	Well, Mr Tomkins isn't here yet, but he's told me that we *don't need to* [0] wait for him, so let's start. What _____ we _____ [1] do before Saturday?
PUPIL 1	We _____ [2] mark out the playground so that each class has enough space for its exhibition. Most of the classes _____ [3] much space but one of them _____ [4] a bigger area because they've got a big display.
PUPIL 2	We _____ [5] decorations for the corridors. We _____ [6] put them up before Friday, but we certainly _____ [7] make them before then. We'll tell all the classes.
PUPIL 1	And someone _____ [8] order drinks and crisps and everything. I can do that if you like.
TEACHER	All right. And you have to choose someone to make a short speech. It _____ [9] be someone with a strong voice.
PUPIL 2	We _____ [10] choose anyone because Isabella has already volunteered.
TEACHER	That sounds just like Isabella.

F   Storm warning

Very heavy rains are forecast for the next few days. Read the weather warning, and complete it by crossing out one of the two options in each case.

Recent experience of storms shows that everybody *needs/~~must~~* [0] to play their part to avoid major problems. In general, if you *mustn't/don't have to* [1] go out, then you *should/need* [2] stay at home. As for school pupils, if public transport is not affected, then they *must/need* [3] attend school as usual, but if the journey looks dangerous, they *mustn't/don't have to* [4] take any risks to reach school. Working adults *ought/must* [5] decide on the best way to get to work, but anyone who is driving and comes to a flooded river, *must/has* [6] not attempt to cross it. You *mustn't/don't have to* [7] switch off your electricity and gas at the mains now, but if your house starts to flood, you *shouldn't/must* [8] do this immediately. You *mustn't/should* [9] listen to the radio to hear any flood warnings and houses that are at risk *ought to/don't have to* [10] have sandbags ready to block doors.

OVER TO YOU Now go to page 123.

1 Some verbs are usually followed by an **infinitive**:
We've arranged to meet tomorrow.
We're planning to have a party.
I promised to call her tonight.

We use an **infinitive** after these verbs:

afford	agree	aim	arrange	begin
decide	deserve	expect	fail	hope
intend	learn	manage	need	offer
plan	pretend	promise	refuse	seem
start	threaten	want		

We make a negative sentence with **not**:
She managed not to lose her keys this time.
He pretended not to hear.

2 Some verbs are usually followed by an **-ing form**:
Do you enjoy flying?
I hate getting wet.

We use an **-ing form** after these verbs:

admit	adore	avoid	can't stand
consider	deny	dislike	don't mind
enjoy	escape	fancy	feel like	finish
imagine	involve	keep (on)	look forward to
mention	mind	miss	practise	regret
resist	suggest	understand	

Grammar in action

1 We can use verbs such as **aim**, **arrange**, **hope**, **plan** + **infinitive** to talk about arrangements:
We aim to arrive around 7 p.m., then we've arranged to meet some old friends for dinner, so we hope to see you after that.

2 We often use verbs about intentions and decisions followed by the **infinitive** to explain why we do things:
Chris decided to buy Anne some flowers.

3 We can describe our likes and dislikes with many verbs that take an **-ing form**. Here, someone is looking back over their holiday:
I really enjoyed seeing the Taj Mahal, and I loved eating so much spicy food. But I disliked being so hot all the time.

A   Making holiday arrangements

Read this holiday advertisement. Use the verbs in brackets, in the correct form, to complete the information.

Have you decided where to go on holiday this year?

We promise ___to help___ ⁰ (help) you decide.

Do you enjoy _____¹ (cycle) in the countryside and _____² (walk) in the mountains?

If you fancy _____³ (escape) from the crowds and _____⁴ (do) something different,

and you don't mind _____⁵ (share) your holiday with others, we offer _____⁶ (show)

you the most fantastic places. If you can't afford _____⁷ (spend) a lot of money, don't worry!

We promise _____⁸ (beat) any price offered by our competitors.

We always aim _____⁹ (give) our clients the best possible holiday experience.

Contact us on 01632 960893 for more information about our fantastic range of holidays.

And you just need _____¹⁰ (mention) this advertisement to get an extra discount!

B Big decisions

Complete the dialogue with the correct form of the verb in brackets:

MATT What are you hoping _to do_ ⁰ (do) after you leave school?

CLAIRE Well, I'm planning .... ¹ (spend) some time relaxing, but I've promised .... ² (look) properly at whether I'd like .... ³ (go) to university or whether I want .... ⁴ (find) a job.

MATT Don't you have to plan .... ⁵ (study) at university before you finish school - a year in advance?

CLAIRE You certainly can arrange .... ⁶ (start) at university straight after school, but I've always hoped .... ⁷ (work) abroad as an English teacher before continuing my studies. My parents seem .... ⁸ (encourage) me and my brother to be independent: I intended .... ⁹ (organize) something soon, but they suggested .... ¹⁰ (take) some time off while I think about my decisions.

MATT That sounds amazing! My parents said that I needed .... ¹¹ (decide) about my plans before I finished school. They wanted me to enjoy .... ¹² (work) in a job, so they suggested .... ¹³ (organize) some work experience over the holiday. I really enjoyed .... ¹⁴ (meet) the people and .... ¹⁵ (earn) my own money, so when the company offered me a full-time job, I accepted straight away!

WORD FOCUS

Find words in exercise B that have these meanings:

A in a different country

....

B agreed to take

....

C Explaining why we do things

A major supermarket is planning to charge shoppers for plastic carrier bags. Read these comments posted on a website. Use the verbs in the box to complete the gaps.

| plan | use | avoid | take |

'I think it's almost impossible to _avoid using_ ⁰ plastic bags when you go shopping. I always .... ¹ a bag with me, but I usually forget.'— Dave, Oxford.

| pay | refuse | need | think |

'People .... ² about the planet. We should all .... ³ for these bags and bring our own.'— Jeanne, Birmingham.

| shop | manage | put | go |

'We all .... ⁴ every week. If we plan ahead, we can all .... ⁵ some bags in the car before we go to the supermarket.'— Kazumi, Cambridge.

| make | raise | keep on | hope |

'I think the problem here is that the supermarkets .... ⁶ a lot of money by selling bags. They .... ⁷ prices and everything is more expensive.'— Sandra, Edinburgh.

| decide | go | threaten | change |

'The best solution is for everyone to .... ⁸ to another supermarket, then they will quickly .... ⁹ this stupid policy.'— Martin, Cardiff.

3 We can use some verbs with a person as object + infinitive, e.g.:

> I **want my son to learn** Russian.
> Will you **encourage them to take** part?
> Jack **helped me to mend** my bike.

Notice that when the person is in the form of a pronoun, it is the object form: **me, him, her, us, them.**

We use these verbs in this structure:

allow	ask	cause	encourage	expect	force
get	help	invite	leave	like	love	need
prefer	persuade	teach	tell	train	want

> TIP
>
> These verbs always take an object:
> **dare, encourage, force, invite, order, persuade, remind, teach, tell, warn.**
>> She taught **me** to play the piano.
>> He's invited **his parents** to go with him.

4 Now look at these examples. We can use **make** (= force), **let** (= allow) and **help** + person with a verb (infinitive without **to**):

> The police didn't **make her sign** anything.
> Will you **let the children come** with us?

Grammar in action

4 We can use **advise, ask, beg, challenge, encourage, instruct, invite, order, persuade, remind, request, teach, tell, urge, warn** + object + infinitive to talk about how one person influences another:

> My teacher encouraged me to apply for university, but she warned me not to be too hopeful.

5 We use **allow, enable, forbid, permit** and **require** + object + infinitive, and **let** + verb to explain what is permitted or allowed:

> They won't allow you to cycle here.
> This pass will enable you to enter the premises.

D How I became a rock star

The famous rock star, Zak Gellar, is describing how he began his career in music. Re-write the sentences using the verbs given.

0 My teacher said I should listen to more music. (encourage)

My teacher encouraged me to listen to more music.

1 My brother showed me how to play the guitar. (teach)

....

2 My mother thought I would go to university. (expect)

....

3 My father said to me, 'You should study engineering.' (want)

....

4 When I first met my manager, he said, 'Please give me a chance.' (persuade)

....

5 My manager showed me how to get a record deal. (help)

....

6 The famous musicians, 'The Rolling Faces', said to me, 'Please join our tour.' (invite)

....

E Miranda's school report

Complete Miranda's school report by forming sentences using the words in brackets and adding *to* where necessary.

Class Teacher's comments:

Miranda has had a very mixed year. As you know, we *have allowed her to study* ⁰ (have allowed / study / her) four subjects instead of three this year. However, we haven't _____ ¹ (let / her / choose) those subjects. We have also _____ ² (her / permitted / study) at home on Mondays. We therefore _____ ³ (expected / her / do) much better than she has.

Art Teacher's comments:

What a fantastic year for Miranda! She _____ ⁴ (deserves / be) top of the class! I would seriously _____ ⁵ (apply / encourage / her) for Art School in the future. Although, clearly we can't _____ ⁶ (her / make / go) to college if she doesn't want to.

Geography Teacher's comments:

Poor Miranda! What a disappointing year! I'm afraid I must _____ ⁷ (remind / you / aim) higher. And, try to _____ ⁸ (let / me / help) you sometimes.

Headteacher's comments:

I must _____ ⁹ (you / warn / work) harder next year!

F Sean's new bicycle

Read what happened to Sean's new bicycle. There are mistakes in the eleven phrases underlined. Rewrite the phrases, correcting the mistakes.

<u>Sean's parents bought him a new bicycle ride</u>
Sean's parents bought him a new bicycle to ride ⁰ to school.
<u>They encouraged to him to take</u> _____ ¹ a lock for the bicycle, because <u>they didn't want anyone steal</u> _____ ² it.
On the first day, <u>they reminded to take Sean</u> _____ ³ the lock to school. But, unfortunately Sean was very forgetful, so <u>he failed take</u> _____ ⁴ the lock with him. When he arrived at school, he left the bicycle outside the classroom.

When Sean finished class, <u>he it expected to be</u> _____ ⁵ there. But it wasn't! Someone had taken it. <u>His friends him helped look</u> _____ ⁶ for it, but they couldn't find it. <u>They decided him to call</u> _____ ⁷ the police, and <u>they Sean persuaded to tell</u> _____ ⁸ his parents what had happened. They were annoyed with Sean because <u>they had warned not to forget</u> _____ ⁹ the lock. After that, <u>they wouldn't let Sean to take</u> _____ ¹⁰ anything new to school.

OVER TO YOU Now go to page 123.

10 Infinitives and *-ing* forms (2)
I like to play tennis or *I like playing tennis*

1 Some verbs can take an **infinitive** or an *-ing* form, with the same meaning:

> begin   continue   hate   intend
> like   love   prefer   start

*I **like to go** for long walks.*
*I **like going** for long walks.*
*The waiters **continued to clear** the tables.*
*The waiters **continued clearing** the tables.*

> **TIP**
> Notice that **would hate / would like / would love / would prefer** are always followed by an infinitive with **to**.

2 We can use an **infinitive** or an *-ing* form with these verbs, but with a change of meaning:

> try   remember   forget   stop

*I **tried to see** Mary but she was in a meeting.*
(= I made an attempt/I did my best to see Mary.)
*If you can't get to sleep, **try counting** sheep.*
(= Experiment to see if counting sheep helps.)

*Did you **remember to buy** some bread?*
(= Remember first, then do something.)
*Do you **remember going** to London when you were 3?*
(= Do something, then you remember it.)

*I **forgot to phone** your sister.*
(= I didn't remember to phone.)
*I'll never **forget seeing** Rio de Janeiro for the first time.*
(= I will always have a memory of seeing Rio.)

*I was walking home from school and **stopped to play** football.*
(= I stopped so that I could play football.)
*I **stopped playing** football two years ago, when I broke my leg.*
(= I played football in the past, but I don't play now.)

Grammar in action

1 We can use **can't bear**, **can't stand**, **hate**, **like**, **love** and **prefer + infinitive** or *-ing* form to talk about our likes and dislikes, feelings and preferences:

> *I can't bear waiting at bus stops and I can't stand to stand in a queue.* (= I don't like waiting and I hate to stand in a queue.)

2 We use **stop + infinitive** or *-ing* form to talk about the order things happen in:

> *Emma stopped to talk to Maria.*
> (= She stopped what she was doing to talk to her.)
> *Emma stopped talking to Maria.* (= She talked to her, and then she finished.)

A   Infinitive or *-ing* form?

Cross out the incorrect form in these sentences.

0 Have you seen my hat? ~ Yes, I remember *seeing / to see* it in the kitchen yesterday.

1 *The End of Reason* is a fantastic film. You must remember *seeing / to see* it when you get a chance.

2 I can't stop *thinking / to think* about the book I read last night - it was very moving.

3 What would you like for dinner? ~ I have too much work to do - I can't stop *thinking / to think* about food!

4 I would love *going / to go* for a walk this afternoon.

5 I mustn't forget *showing / to show* you my photographs tomorrow.

6 I'll never forget *showing / to show* my father the painting I did of him - he thought it was terrible!

B The weekend's visit

Ewan is planning to visit his brother, Matt. Read his letter and complete the sentences using the verbs given.

Hi Matt,

Just a quick letter about the weekend. I've _tried to contact_ ⁰ (try / contact) you by email several times, but you didn't reply, so I've .... ¹ (stop / try).

I'll be there on Saturday, and I would .... ² (like / see) some of my old school friends. You know I really .... ³ (like / play) football with them in the park. Can you .... ⁴ (remember / contact) them all to say I'm coming? Or, if they would .... ⁵ (prefer / watch) a match, we can go to the stadium. Do you .... ⁶ (remember / go) to that match when I came to see you at Christmas? We all .... ⁷ (try / not cry) when our team lost, but it was impossible. I've .... ⁸ (stop / support) them now, as they played so badly that day.

What about Jamie, has he .... ⁹ (stop / grow) yet? I remember he was nearly six feet tall when he was 12! He said he .... ¹⁰ (hate / be) so tall. Has his sister, Katie .... ¹¹ (start / like) football yet? You can tell me all the news when I get there.

OK, that's it for now. Don't .... ¹² (forget / meet) me at the station on Saturday at six o' clock!

See you soon,

Ewan

C Anita's blog

Read Anita's blog. Use the verbs in the box in the correct form to complete the sentences.

tell   talk   model   get   relax   do   work   study   go   be   set

Bad start to the day! Didn't remember _to set_ ⁰ the alarm and I forgot .... ¹ Mum I had to get up early. So I was late for school again. That's the third time this week. You may think I don't like school, but believe it or not, I actually love .... ² to school! But I suppose I would prefer not .... ³ all the time. I would like .... ⁴ sometimes and do nothing for a change. I also hate .... ⁵ all these exams!

If I wasn't at school, I would love .... ⁶ as a model like my friend Jasmine. In the future, I want to work in fashion and I tried .... ⁷ once in order to get some experience. I didn't have very much success, though.

Anyway, I tried .... ⁸ to my teacher when I finally got to school to explain, but she was too busy. When I saw her later, she said that if I continued .... ⁹ late every day she would tell my mum and dad. What can I do? I must do my best to get up early tomorrow and try .... ¹⁰ to school on time!

3 We can use the *-ing* form of a verb as the subject of a sentence:

> ***Driving*** *isn´t easy.*
> *Does* ***swimming*** *strengthen your back?*

These subjects can have their own objects and adverbs, e.g.:

> ***Driving a lorry*** *isn't easy.*
> *Does* ***swimming regularly*** *strengthen your back?*

We can also say:

> *My favourite sport is* ***windsurfing****.*
> *My daughter's hobby is* ***painting****.*

4 Adjective + infinitive
We can use this structure after the verbs **be, seem, appear, look**:

> *She's* ***afraid to speak*** *to him.*
> *He* ***looked pleased to see*** *us.*

Common adjectives in this pattern are:

> afraid   annoyed   curious   delighted
> difficult   easy   funny   great   happy
> hard   impossible   likely   nice   pleased
> right   sad   sorry   surprised   unlikely
> wonderful   wrong

> **TIP**
>
> We often use **verb + adjective + infinitive** after **it**:
> ***It's funny to see*** *my sister on TV.*
> (NOT USUALLY *To see my sister on TV…'*)
>
> ***It's wrong to criticize*** *him.*

5 Adjective + preposition + *-ing* form
Look at these examples:

> *Our daughter's* ***afraid of flying****.*
> *We were very* ***excited about going*** *to Chile.*
> *He's not very* ***good at listening*** *to other people's ideas.*
> *Rachel's* ***used to getting up*** *early.* (= She has no problem with getting up early regularly)

Common combinations are:

> afraid of   capable/incapable of
> excited about   fond of
> brilliant/clever/good/hopeless/terrible at
> keen on   interested in   tired of   used to

Grammar in action

3 We use *-ing* forms to express many different activities. Here, we are comparing different sports:

> *My favourite sport is skiing but of course you can only do it in the winter. ~ Running and cycling are what I like best.*

We often use **go** + *-ing* form for sports and other activities:

> *Len goes cycling every Saturday.*
> *We'll have to go shopping tomorrow.*
> *Have you been skiing this year?*

4 Another common use for *-ing* forms is in signs with **no**, to forbid actions that are against the rules:

> *NO WALKING ON THE GRASS!*
> *NO SMOKING!*

5 We can use **adjectives with infinitives** or with a **preposition + *-ing*** form to explain our feelings and reactions:

> *Clare was surprised to see us but she was excited about talking to her cousins because she was interested in finding out how they were doing at school. It was great to chat to her, too.*

or to give opinions and make comments:

> *It's impossible to understand her, but I'm fond of hearing her laugh!*

6 We can describe people's strengths and weaknesses using **adjectives** with a **preposition + *-ing*** form. Here, someone is talking about a colleague at work:

> *She's very good at working in a team, and she's brilliant at planning her work.*

D Job applications

All these people applied for the same job. Look at the notes made at their interviews and write sentences about their strengths and weaknesses. Use a preposition and the correct form of the verb.

Work in a team	Stella	very good
	Robin	hopeless
Use a computer	Robbie and John	afraid
	Martin and Peter	brilliant
Write reports	Helen	very keen
Talk to customers	Rosa	not interested
	Karma	excited
Answer the telephone	Nandeep	terrible
	Hitomi and Ronald	incapable

0 Stella *is very good at working in a team*.

1 Robin ....

2 Robbie and John ....

3 Martin and Peter ....

4 Helen ....

5 Rosa ....

6 Karma ....

7 Nandeep ....

8 Hitomi and Ronald ....

E Holiday memories

Penny and Donna are in a café talking about their holiday. Complete their conversation with the correct form of the verbs from the box.

be	bring	collect	find	remember
see	sit	sunbathe	swim	windsurf

PENNY   It was a wonderful holiday. Just *sitting* ⁰ here in the sunshine reminds me of that little bar near the beach.

DONNA   The beach where we went .... ¹ in the sea?

PENNY   You mean where we tried .... ² and you never managed to get on the board!

DONNA   That's true, but it was fun, anyway, and at least we enjoyed .... ³ on the sand afterwards.

PENNY   Yes, and I'm glad we weren't in the water when that shark appeared. Imagine .... ⁴ a shark's lunch!

DONNA   I don't think it was a shark, but I'll never forget .... ⁵ everybody race out of the water. They all wanted to avoid .... ⁶ out if it was a shark or not. Did you remember .... ⁷ your photos to show me?

PENNY   No, I forgot .... ⁸ them from the shop.

DONNA   You're hopeless at .... ⁹ the most important things in life!

Find phrases in exercise E that have these meanings:

A leave the water very quickly

....

B discovering

....

OVER TO YOU Now go to page 123.

11 The passive
Present and past tenses

1 The object in the active sentence corresponds to the subject in the passive sentence:

All schools teach │ maths. │ (OBJECT)

│ Maths │ (SUBJECT) is taught in all schools.

2 We make the **passive** form with auxiliary verb **be** + **past participle**. The form of **be** changes person (1st, 2nd, 3rd) and tense. The past participle always stays the same:

Present simple:	All letters **are typed**.
Present continuous:	The house is **being painted**.
Past simple:	The school **was built** in 1978.
Past continuous:	The grass **was being cut**.
Present perfect:	The car **has been repaired**.
Past perfect:	The table **had been reserved**.

We form negatives and questions in the same way as in active sentences:

The game **isn't being televised** tonight.
The party **hasn't been organized**.
Were the windows **being cleaned**?
Had the decision **been made** when you arrived?

(For a list of irregular past participles, see p. 129.)

3 We can mention the agent (the person / thing that did the action) in a passive sentence with **by** + **noun**:

Hamlet *was written* **by Shakespeare**.

4 We can use the **passive** when the person/thing that did an action is not relevant, or not known:

What is paper made from? ~ It's made from wood.

Usually we do not need to mention the agent in a passive sentence. We do not mention it if it is not important for the meaning of the sentence:

The house was built ~~by some builders~~ in 1888.
(We do not need to say 'by some builders' as this does not give any new information.)

Grammar in action

1 We can use the **passive** to talk about processes, for example scientific or historical processes:

Originally iron was made using a wood fire, but later steel was produced in a furnace that burnt coal. Nowadays most of our steel is imported.

2 We often use the **passive** in formal writing to sound impersonal. This example is from a newspaper report:

The country has been affected by flooding; hundreds of people have been evacuated; many still need to be airlifted to higher ground.

3 We use the **passive** with **by** if we want to focus on the subject of the passive sentence. This might be so that the sentence connects better with the one before. This is useful in extended written and spoken descriptions, such as this guided tour:

We're now in Endigate Street. This street was designed by famous architects who were empoyed directly by the King.
('This street' links to the previous sentence.)

Or it might be because the sentence would not make sense without mentioning the agent.

The theatre was designed by Hawksmoor. ('The theatre was designed' would not make sense.)

A Food production

Write complete sentences about food production using the verb in the present simple passive.

0 Cheese / produce / from milk.

Cheese is produced from milk.

1 Grapes / grow / in many countries. About half / eat / as fruit and half / make / into wine.

....

2 Nowadays, most fruit / wash / before it / sell / to the public.

....

3 At sea, fish / freeze / as soon as they / catch.

....

4   Some fish / keep / in fish farms. They / feed / with food that / produce / in a factory.

....

5   Oranges / often / pick / when they are green because they / transport / thousands of miles.

....

6   Flour / make / from cereal grains such as wheat and rye. It / use / to make bread
    and cakes.

....

B   Historical events

**Make questions and answers in the past simple passive using a verb
from the first column and a person from the second column.**

build	Usain Bolt, a Jamaican athlete
compose	Alexander Fleming, a Scottish scientist
discover	John Logie Baird, a Scottish inventor
invent	~~John Lennon, an English popstar~~
paint	Leonardo da Vinci, an Italian artist
win	J. K. Rowling, a British author
write	the ancient Egyptians

0   'Imagine'   *Who was 'Imagine' composed by? It was composed by John Lennon, an English popstar.*

1   the Mona Lisa ....

2   penicillin ....

3   the television ....

4   the Harry Potter books ....

5   the 100m sprint at the Beijing Olympics ....

6   the pyramids ....

C   A fire at the school

Rewrite the sentences using the passive.

0   They'd already served dinner at the school.

Dinner had already been served at the school.

1   A few minutes later, someone found a fire in the
    school kitchen.

....

2   The fire started because someone had left a
    cooker on.

....

3   They notified the fire brigade a few minutes ago.

....

4   They've evacuated the school.

....

5   Someone has counted all the students.

....

6   They're checking the school to make sure no one is
    still inside.

....

7   They're allowing the students to go home early.

....

11 The passive
Future and modal passives; *have something done*

5 Future and modal passives

We use **be + past participle** after **will, be going to, must, should, have to**, etc. for the future and modal verbs in the passive:

The future
He'**ll be invited** back next year.
Those trees **are going to be cut** down.
Is she **going to be offered** the job?

Modal verbs
Doors **must be locked** at the end of the day.
The letters **should be checked** before they are sent out.
The cheques **have to be signed** by two people.

6

Some verbs can have two objects, e.g. **ask, give, lend, offer, pay, promise, sell, send, show, teach, tell**. With these verbs, we usually make the indirect object of an active sentence the subject of a passive sentence:

ACTIVE: *An ex-spy taught* **Jack** *Russian.* [INDIRECT OBJECT: Jack]
PASSIVE: **Jack** *was taught Russian by an ex-spy.* [SUBJECT: Jack]

A person can often be the subject in a passive sentence with these verbs:
Lily was given some chocolates.
Mike has been promised more money.

7 Have something done

We can also form passive-type sentences like this:

have + object + past participle

Present simple:	I **have my hair cut** every six weeks.
Present continuous:	He's **having his car serviced** today.
Past simple:	Sally **had her eyes tested**.
Present perfect:	You'**ve had your windows cleaned**.
Going to:	They'**re going to have their bedroom painted**.
Modal verb:	I **must have my shoes mended**.

The subject is the person who <u>decided</u>, not who did the action. Compare:
Our neighbours are painting their house.
(= They are doing the painting themselves.)
*Our neighbours **are having their house painted**.*
(= Someone is painting the house for the neighbours.)

> We can also use **get + object + past participle**, in informal situations:
> *Where do you **get your car serviced**?*
> TIP

Grammar in action

4
We can use the **passive** to talk in a factual way about official plans and decisions:
The town centre is going to be re-designed next year as a pedestrian area. Private traffic will be excluded and a regular bus service will be introduced.

5
We often use **have/get something done** to talk from the point of view of a customer about professional services, such as haircuts, building work, dental work, etc. **Get** is more informal:
Jeevan had his tooth taken out yesterday.
We're getting an extension built on the garage.

D The life of a film star

Complete the sentences about the film star Jemima Joseph's life using a form of *have something done*. Use the correct tense each time.

0 The shops deliver all Jemima's shopping each week.
Jemima has all her shopping delivered each week.

1 Someone else answers all her fan mail.
She ....

2 Last week, a hairdresser coloured Jemima's hair.

Last week, she ....

3 A photographer is going to take Jemima's photo next Friday.

She .... next Friday.

4 Last year, a designer made a special dress for Jemima, for the Oscars.

Jemima .... for the Oscars last year.

5 A reporter suggested that a dentist has whitened Jemima's teeth.

A reporter suggested that Jemima ....

6 Some people are decorating her flat.

At the moment, she ....

E   Changes at the school

At a school meeting, the teachers talk about changes. Complete the text by putting in the correct form of the verbs in brackets.

MRS SMITH   Well, now that the new extension has *been completed*⁰ (complete) and the new computers ....¹ (install), we can look at other changes that ....² (need).

MR JONES   How much money can ....³ (spend) this year?

MRS SMITH   Well, last year, as you know, the school ....⁴ (give) just over £15,000 to cover running costs. This year, the final figure isn't going to ....⁵ (decide) until July, but it ....⁶ (expect) to be around £17,000.

MR TIMMS   We ....⁷ (promise) more than that at the beginning of the year.

MS SLATER   That was before the municipal elections. What politicians say before the elections can't always ....⁸ (trust).

MRS SMITH   Anyway, what's urgent? Last year, we .... the classrooms ....⁹ (have/paint). What should we ....¹⁰ (have/do) this year?

MR TIMMS   I think we should .... the heating system ....¹¹. (have/check) Some rooms were quite cold last winter.

MRS SMITH   That sounds sensible and it would only take up about half of the budget. What else?

MR JONES   What about the old ovens in the kitchen? Shouldn't they ....¹² (replace)?

MS SLATER   Quite right! The cooks ....¹³ (tell) long ago that the ovens would be the top of the list.

MRS SMITH   Well, that means that not much money will ....¹⁴ (leave) over for other things. We'd better find out how much these two things will cost before any other decisions ....¹⁵ (take).

OVER TO YOU Now go to page 123.

A *budget* is a sum of money reserved for a particular purpose.

WORD FOCUS

1 **Phrasal verbs** have two parts: a verb (e.g. **look**) and an adverb (e.g. **up**, **out**):

> Ken **looked up** the new words in his dictionary.
> You'll have an accident if you don't **look out**.
> What time do we have to **check in**?

2 Some phrasal verbs have an object:

> Mike threw away **his old jeans**.
> May I take off **my jacket**?

When the object is a noun (e.g. **his old jeans**), it can come before or after the adverb:

> Mike **threw** his old jeans **away**.
> OR Mike **threw away** his old jeans.
> May I **take** my jacket **off**? OR May I **take off** my jacket?

When the object is a pronoun (e.g. **them**), it must come after the verb and before the adverb:

> Ken **threw** them **away**.
> May I **take** it **off**?

3 Some common phrasal verbs that have an object are:

> call back/off   drop off   fill in (a form)
> find out   give up (= stop doing)   hand in
> look up (in a dictionary, etc.)   make up
> pick up   put away/down/off/on/up   sort out
> take off (clothes)   tell off   throw away
> tire out   try on   turn down/up (TV, stereo)
> switch/turn on/off (lights, TV)

4 Some phrasal verbs do not have an object:

> You'll have an accident if you don't **look out**.
> What time do we have to **check in** at the airport?
> Emily **isn't in** at the moment.
> During the week I **get up** at 7 o'clock.

5 Some common phrasal verbs that do not have an object are:

> be in/out/away/back   fall out (= argue)
> get up, give in / give up (= admit defeat)
> go/carry on (= continue)   go out (= do something for entertainment)
> hang on / hold on (= wait)   look out (= pay attention)   set off = (leave)   shut up (= be quiet)   take off (= leave the ground)

> They used to be friends but they've **fallen out**.
> What time are you going to **set off**?

The meaning of a phrasal verb is often different from the meaning of the verb and adverb alone, e.g. **look up** = consult, **look out** = be careful, **call off** = cancel. You cannot usually guess the meaning, and should use a learner's dictionary instead.

Grammar in action

1 In informal English, we often use a phrasal verb where in formal English we would use a single verb, e.g. **find out** (informal) = discover (formal), **sort out** = arrange, **set off** = leave. For example, we might talk to a friend about a trip:

> Did you find out when we need to set off? ~ Yes, I've sorted it all out.

A   Everyday exchanges

Complete each of these short dialogues by adding an object + an adverb.

0   Has the match been cancelled? ~ Yes, they called ....it off........ yesterday.

1   Do you think this skirt will fit Sara? ~ I don't know. I'll get her to try ....

2   One of us has to collect Peter from school. ~ OK. I'll pick ....

3   Have we still got that old lamp? ~ No, I threw .... last week.

4   Aren't you too warm in those boots? ~ Yes, I think I'll take ....

5   The music's very loud. ~ OK. I'll turn .... a bit.

6   How long do we have for the projects? ~ We have to hand .... on Friday.

7   Who invented that stupid story? ~ I think he made .... himself.

8   Have you got any cigarettes? ~ No, my doctor told me to give ....

9 Are you busy? ~ Yes, I am. Can I call .... later?

10 What time did you get home? ~ The taxi dropped .... at 1.30.

B Arriving at a hotel

Sue Nopes is staying at a hotel on a business trip. Complete the text using the phrasal verbs from the list. Include the pronouns and nouns in brackets.

| check in | dress up | fill in | get up | give up | go on | hang on |
| look up | set off | sort out | take off | tire out | turn off |

RECEPTIONIST Hello, Ms. Nopes. Nice to see you again. Have you had a good flight?

SUE Well, I _set off_ ⁰ from home at half past five because I had to get to the airport to .... ¹ before 6 o'clock. But at least the plane .... ² on time, so it was all right.

RECEPTIONIST That's fine. You don't need to bother with the form. I'll .... ³ (it) for you. Would you like a non-smoking room?

SUE Yes, I .... ⁴ smoking last winter when I had such a terrible cold.

RECEPTIONIST It'll be room 504. We had a bit of trouble with the temperature there yesterday but I think they've .... ⁵ the air conditioning now.

SUE I can't stand air conditioning. I always .... ⁶ (it) as soon as I get into the room. Incidentally, we're having dinner at the Oriole restaurant. Do you know where it is?

RECEPTIONIST Please .... ⁷ just a moment. I'll .... ⁸ the address for you.

SUE It's with work colleagues so I won't have to .... ⁹ specially for it, but it'll probably .... ¹⁰ until midnight.

RECEPTIONIST That's a long day. Here we are – 25 Jermin Street.

SUE Thanks. Yes, these long days .... ¹¹ (me) but at least I won't have to .... ¹² early tomorrow morning because my flight back doesn't leave until half past eleven.

C Mother and children

A mother is complaining to a friend about her teenage children. Complete the text by filling each gap with one of the words in the box.

| away | carry | fall | give | go | on | on | out |
| out | pick | put | shut | turn | up | up | up |

They are so untidy. They never _pick_ ⁰ their things _up_ ⁰ or .... ¹ their clothes .... ² in the cupboards. Some days they are the best of friends, but then they .... ³ .... ⁴ and argue and tell each other to .... ⁵ .... ⁶. And they always seem to .... ⁷ the television .... ⁸ when I'm talking on the phone so I can't hear what the other person's saying. Or they .... ⁹ .... ¹⁰ to see their friends without saying where they are going. Sometimes I feel ready to .... ¹¹ .... ¹² altogether, but then I realize that most parents have these problems and we all simply have to .... ¹³ .... ¹⁴.

6 Prepositional verbs have two parts: a verb (e.g. **look**) and a preposition (e.g. **at**, **after**)
> Come and **look at** the sunset.
> Who's **looking after** the baby?
> Can you **deal with** Ms. Turner?

7 Prepositional verbs always have an object; the object can be a noun (e.g. **Ms. Turner**) or a pronoun (e.g. **her**).
> Do you **believe in** ghosts?
> **Wait for** us!

The object always comes after the preposition.
> NOT *Do you believe ghosts in?*
> NOT *Wait us for!*

8 The meaning of a prepositional verb is sometimes easy to guess:
> I'll **pay for** the drinks.
> The exam **consists of** three parts.

However, sometimes the meaning is different from the meanings of the two parts:
> I **came across** an old friend. (= met)
> Do you see what I'm **getting at**? (= trying to explain)

Some common prepositional verbs are:

> apply for   ask for   believe in   belong to
> call for/at/on   come across   consist of
> deal with   feel like   get at/over   laugh at
> listen to   look for/into/after   pay for
> stand for   talk about   think about/of   wait for

9 There are also a few verbs that have three parts:

> catch up with   get away with   get on with
> go out with   live up to   look down on
> look forward to   look up to   put up with
> run out of

These verbs always have an object:
> I'm **looking forward to** your visit.
> How can you **put up with** it?

It is often difficult to understand the meaning of three-part verbs from the meaning of the parts:
> Do you **get on with** your colleagues?
> (= have a friendly relationship with)
> She **looks up to** her older sister.
> (= admires and respects)

Grammar in action

2 We often use prepositional verbs in informal situations – for example, when talking to friends or family:
> I **ran into** my nephew the other day.
> He really **takes after** my brother.

> **TIP**
> The phrase **I look forward to hearing from you** is useful in formal letters when we expect a reply.

D   Email to a friend

Below is an email from one friend to another. Put the words in the correct order to make sentences.

0 (email / for / Thank you / your)   Thank you for your email.

1 (getting / glad / I'm / infection / over / you're / your) ....

2 (Sally / Is / after / you / looking ?) ....

3 (You / like / visitors / feel / at / moment / won't / the) ....

4 (London / call / come / on / to / us / when / you / But) ....

5 (forward / looking / seeing / to / We're / you) ....

E Looking for a volunteer

Complete the dialogue using the correct form of two words from the box in each gap.

> about   after   ~~belong~~   consist   deal   find   for   for   for
> look   look   of   out   pay   stand   think   ~~to~~   with

JAMES   You know that I ___belong to___ ⁰ a charity organization.

BILL   Oh, yes. What's it called?

JAMES   EAT. It .... ¹ European Animal Treatment. We try to
.... ² some groups of endangered animals. Well, we're
.... ³ a part-time volunteer. I thought you might be interested.

BILL   What does the job .... ⁴?

JAMES   The person will have to .... ⁵ emails and answer the phone.
Perhaps write some letters. Of course, EAT will .... ⁶ the stamps
and anything else you need. If you want to .... ⁷ more about it,
you can go to the website.

BILL   It sounds interesting. I'll certainly .... ⁸ it.

F Trouble at work

**Carol tells Alice about her problems. Complete the dialogue by putting in the correct
form of one of the verbs from the box, and include the words in brackets.**

> apply for   ask for   break down   carry on   feel like   fill in
> find out   get away with   ~~get on~~   get on with   look for
> put away   put off   put up with   run out of   tell off

WORD FOCUS

**Find phrases in
exercise F that have
these meanings:**

A   avoids doing
them until later

....

B   avoid the
consequences

ALICE   Well, Carol – how are you ___getting on___ ⁰ in your job?

CAROL   Not very well. I don't really .... ¹ my boss at all. I can't
.... ² his lazy way of doing things. He does things when he
.... ³ (it) rather than when we need it and as for decisions, he
always .... ⁴ (them) until the last minute.

ALICE   How does he .... ⁵ (it)? Doesn't anyone .... ⁶
(him)?

CAROL   Well, he plays golf with one of the directors. Anyway, last week he told me the
photocopier had .... ⁷ and asked me to .... ⁸
what had happened.

ALICE   And what was the problem?

CAROL   Nothing, it had simply .... ⁹ ink. And I .... ¹⁰
some new ink supplies two weeks ago. I followed the normal procedure
by .... ¹¹ an order form and taking it to him but he just
.... ¹² (it) in one of his drawers. And obviously he never sent it.

ALICE   I think you should .... ¹³ a new job, because you can't
.... ¹⁴ like this.

CAROL   I know. I've already started looking. I .... ¹⁵ two jobs last week, but
so far I haven't heard anything.

ALICE   Well, good luck!

OVER TO YOU   Now go to page 123.

13 Indirect speech (1)
Reporting statements

1 We can report what someone said in two ways: direct speech and indirect speech. When we use direct speech, we use the exact words that someone says. When we use indirect speech we give the meaning of the words, but not the exact words:

Ruby said 'I love you, Ben.' (direct)
Ruby said (that) she loved Ben. (indirect)
Ruby told Ben that she loved him. (indirect)

2 In **indirect speech**, we usually use a past reporting verb (e.g. **said**) and we often change the tense of the original verb:

*Toby said, 'We **are meeting** at my flat.'*
*Toby said (that) they **were meeting** at his flat.*

Here are examples of some typical tense changes:

present → past
am/is/are → was/were   take → took
is taking → were taking

present perfect → past perfect
have taken → had taken

past simple → past perfect
took → had taken

modals
will → would   must → had to   can → could
may → might   should → should   would → would
could → could

3 In **indirect speech**, we often change pronouns and possessives to keep the same meaning:

*Toby said, '**We** are meeting at **my** flat.'* (direct)
*Toby said (that) **they** were meeting at **his** flat.* (indirect)

4 We often have to change expressions of time and place:

*Sara said, 'We're leaving **tomorrow**.'*
*Sara told me that they were leaving **the next day**.*

Here are some typical changes of this sort:

direct	indirect
here	there
this	that
today	that day
yesterday	the previous day / the day before
tomorrow	the next/following day / the day after
next month, etc.	the following month / the month after, etc.
last month, etc.	the previous month / the month before, etc.
three days ago	three days before/earlier
come	go

5 In indirect speech, **say** does not have an indirect object but **tell** must have one:

Ruby said that she loved him.
Ruby told Ben/him that she loved him.
NOT *Ruby said Ben/him that she loved him.*
NOT *Ruby told that she loved him.*

> We sometimes use **to** after **say** like this:
> *What did Ruby **say to** him?*
> *Ruby wanted to **say** something **to** Ben.*
>
> TIP

Grammar in action

1 **Indirect speech** is often used by reporters in the media:

Yesterday evening, film stars Nelson Faulkes and Amy Skelp told our reporter that they were going to get married next week.

2 We often use **indirect speech** to tell someone else what we have heard in a talk or speech:

The lecturer said that global warming would be the main issue in mid-century politics.

We also use **indirect speech** to tell someone about something we have read. We can use verbs such as **said** even though we are talking about writing:

In his Times *column, Wilson said that At Gloaming was the best film he had seen for a long time.*

3 We often use **indirect speech** when we gossip with friends, family and colleagues:

That guy in HR said he didn't like the new manager at all, but I think she's OK.

A   Voicemail messages

Lizzie has eight voicemail messages. Below are some of the things her friends left on her voicemail. Complete the sentences to show what she said to her boyfriend about the messages, changing the tenses, pronouns, and possessives.

0   Fred said, 'I need to borrow your ladder.'

Fred said *he needed to borrow our ladder* .

1   Rachel said, 'I'm going to France.'

Rachel said ....

2   Tom said, 'My mother's given me £50.'

Tom told me ....

3   Jane and John said, 'We've moved into our new house.'

Jane and John said ....

4   Sara said, 'I can't finish my essay.'

Sara told me ....

5   Craig said, 'I'll remind John about our meeting.'

Craig told me ....

6   Lena said, 'The parcels arrived safely.'

Lena said ....

B   Moving into a new house

Read the dialogue, then complete the text.

SUZY   Hi, Jane. What are you doing here?

JANE   I'm buying some curtains. We moved into our new house last month and there's lots of work to do.

SUZY   Really?

JANE   Yes, we finished painting the house last week and John cleared the garden yesterday.

JANE   We've got a bit of a problem though. Our new furniture was delivered a couple of weeks ago but I can't arrange it until next week because the carpets haven't arrived. I hope it will look nice when it's finished. My parents are coming to visit us next month.

I saw Jane in the DIY store a few weeks ago. I asked her what she was doing ....*there*.... ⁰ and she said she was buying new curtains. She told me that they'd moved into their new house .... ¹. She said that they'd finished painting it .... ² and that John .... ³ the garden the day before. She explained that their new furniture had been delivered .... ⁴, but she couldn't arrange it until the following week because the carpets .... ⁵. She said she hoped it would look nice when it was all finished, and added that her parents .... ⁶ to visit them .... ⁷.

13

Indirect speech (1)
Reporting questions

6 **Indirect questions** are not real questions so they do not have the word order of questions or a question mark (?):

I said, 'Where does Penny live?' (direct)
*I asked (them) **where Penny lived**. (indirect)*
NOT ~~I asked (them) where did Penny live.~~

Neil said, 'Are you from Sweden?' (direct)
*Neil asked (me) **if I was** from Sweden. (indirect)*
NOT ~~Neil asked (me) was I from Sweden.~~

7 As well as **ask**, we can use **wonder** and **want to know** to report questions, e.g.:

'When will I hear from David?' Liz asked herself.
*Liz **wondered** when she would hear from David.*

'Who has opened my mail?' asked Clare.
*Clare **wanted to know** who had opened her mail.*

8 Many questions begin with a question word (**what**, **where**, etc.). These also appear in the **indirect question**:

'What are you doing, Tim?' said the teacher.
*The teacher asked Tim **what** he was doing.*

'Where does Peter work?' my mother asked.
*My mother asked me **where** Peter worked.*

9 When the original question does not have a question word, the **indirect question** has **if** or **whether**:

'Do you know the answer?' she asked.
*She asked me **if/whether** I knew the answer.*

'Is Isabel Spanish or not?' said Ian.
*Ian asked **if/whether** Isabel was Spanish or not.*

> TIP
>
> We cannot use **say** or **tell** to report indirect questions:
>
> *Bill asked (me) if Sandra was a teacher.*
> NOT ~~Bill said if Sandra was a teacher.~~
> NOT ~~Bill told me if Sandra was a teacher.~~

Grammar in action

4 We can use **indirect questions** to summarize conversations such as job interviews or meetings:

I asked all the candidates if they had university degrees and which languages they could speak. Then I asked them what experience they had and how they felt about working in a team.

C Reporting a meeting

Read the dialogue and then complete how Suki later reported the meeting to a friend. Use *say*, *tell* or *ask* for the reporting verb and standard changes in the tenses.

ERIC   Hello, Suki. What are you doing in Brighton?

SUKI   I came to visit my aunt but I've decided to stay for a couple of days. Do you live here?

ERIC   Yes, I've lived here since 2004. Where do you live?

SUKI   Near Gatwick Airport. I have a small flat there.

ERIC   This afternoon I'm going to the aquarium. Do you want to join me?

SUKI   I can't. Some friends are coming to see us.

ERIC   OK. See you next week at work then.

I saw a colleague called Eric when I went shopping. He _asked_ [0] me _what I was doing_ [0] in Brighton. I _____ [1] him that I _____ [2] to visit my aunt. I also _____ [3] that I _____ [4] to stay for a couple of days. I _____ [5] him _____ [6] in Brighton and he _____ [7] me that he _____ [8] here since 2004. Then he _____ [9] me _____ [10] and I _____ [11] that I _____ [12] a small flat near Gatwick Airport. He _____ [13] me he _____ [14] to the aquarium later and _____ [15] me _____ [16] to join him. I _____ [17] that I _____ [18] because some friends _____ [19] to see us. We'll see each other next week, anyway.

D What happened in the interview?

After leaving school, Zara has an interview for an administrative job. Read the interview and then complete what she said to her parents.

HELEN   Let me start by asking you some questions about school. Did you like school?

ZARA   I enjoyed some subjects more than others. I've always preferred science subjects.

HELEN   Yes, that's clear from your report. But do you have any language qualifications?

ZARA   No, I don't, but I speak French fairly well. You see, my father's French and I often visit my cousins in France.

HELEN   I see. What about hobbies? What do you do in your spare time?

ZARA   I'm a voluntary paramedic.

HELEN   Really? What does a paramedic do?

ZARA   Well, I work at the weekends helping ambulance staff.

HELEN   Did you do a course to become a paramedic?

ZARA   Yes, everybody has to do a course before they can start.

HELEN   I'm not sure that you'd like administrative work. There isn't much opportunity for you to use all of your skills.

ZARA   Are there any other vacancies?

HELEN   The company doctor is looking for a new assistant, I'll speak to him and I'll let you know what he says.

The interviewer asked me _if I had liked school_ [0] and I told
.... [1] some subjects more than
others. I also said .... [2] science
subjects. She asked.. [3] any language
qualifications and I said .... [4]
French fairly well because of you, Dad, and because I often
.... [5] my cousins in France. Then she
asked me .... [6] in my spare time and
I told .... [7] a voluntary paramedic. I
said .... [8] at the weekend with the
ambulance staff. She asked me .... [9]
a course and I told her .... [10] a course
before they .... [11]. At the end of
the interview, she said she .... [12]
sure that .... [13] like administrative
work and she said that there .... [14]
much opportunity for me to use all of my skills. I asked
.... [15] any other vacancies. She said the
company doctor .... [16] an assistant and
she said that .... [17] and let me know
what he .... [18].

OVER TO YOU Now go to page 124.

1 In indirect speech, we use **ask**, **tell** and **advise** like this to report requests, orders and advice:

	verb	+ object	+ infinitive
The secretary	**asked**	us	to fill in the form.
Mr Mills	**told**	the children	to stand up.
The doctor	**advised**	Mr Preston	to exercise.

When the request, order or piece of advice is negative, we add **not** before **to**:

Mr Mills told the children **not** to stand up.

We can use these verbs to explain what people say, but we don't necessarily use their exact words. Other common verbs in this structure are:

> advise forbid invite order persuade
> remind warn

'You really should stop smoking.' → He **advised him to stop smoking**.
'Please come to my party!' ~ 'OK, I will!.' →
I **invited her to come** to my party.
'Don't forget to phone your sister.' → I **reminded him to phone** his sister.
'Don't go near the water!' → She **warned them not to go** near the water.

2 We use these reporting verbs with an infinitive:

> agree offer promise refuse threaten

'OK, I'll tell Jamie.' → She **agreed to tell** Jamie.
'I'll help you.' → He **offered to help** her.

3 We use an **-ing form** after these reporting verbs:

> admit deny suggest

'I got the answer wrong.' → He **admitted getting** the answer wrong.
'No, I didn't touch the mirror.' → He **denied touching** the mirror.
'Why don't we go for a walk?' → He **suggested going** for a walk.

Grammar in action

1 We can use **indirect speech** to report what someone has told us to do. For example, a doctor:

The doctor prescribed some pills for me and told me to take them three times a day. He warned me not to drive after taking them. He suggested not eating very spicy food, and told me to come back in two weeks.

2 We can use **indirect speech** to report what we have told someone else to do. For example, advice we gave to someone about to take an exam:

I told her to keep calm and to read the questions carefully. I reminded her to put her watch on the desk in front of her, and I warned her not to look at other students.

A Reporting what happened in court

In a court of law, the secretary has to note the exact words that are spoken. Based on these notes, complete the newspaper extracts making standard changes in the tenses. Use each reporting verb once.

Female Witness 1:	I saw the suspect stealing my car.
Female Judge:	The witness is making a serious accusation. What do you have to say?
Male Suspect 1:	That's not true.
Female Judge 1:	Speak a bit louder.
Male Suspect 1:	It's not true. I've never stolen a car.

ask   claim   deny   point out   reply   tell

The witness ....._claimed_.....⁰ that she ....._had seen_.....⁰ the suspect stealing
.....................¹ car. The judge ....² that the witness ....³ a
serious accusation and ....⁴ the suspect what he ....⁵ to say.
The suspect ....⁶ that it ....⁷ true. At this point, the judge
.........................⁸ the suspect ....⁹ a bit louder. The suspect went on to
.........................¹⁰ that he ....¹¹ ever stolen a car.

Court official:	Ladies and gentlemen, the judge has been delayed so the trial cannot begin until 11 o' clock.
Judge 2:	The case is complicated and will probably last two or three weeks.
Suspect 2:	But I am totally innocent, your honour, so the case is very simple.
Judge 2:	That is for the court to decide. Now, jury, you must not come to a conclusion until you have heard all the evidence.

announce   declare   explain   point out   instruct

At 10 o' clock, a court official ....¹² that the judge ....¹³
been delayed so the trial ....¹⁴ not begin before 11. When the trial
started, the judge ....¹⁵ to the jury that the case ....¹⁶
complicated and ....¹⁷ probably last two or three weeks. The suspect
then stood up and ....¹⁸ that he ....¹⁹ innocent and said
that the case ....²⁰ very simple. The judge ....²¹ that that
.........................²² for the court to decide. He went on to ....²³ the jury
.........................²⁴ to a conclusion until they ....²⁵ heard all the evidence.

14 Indirect speech (2)
Advanced points

4 When we use **indirect speech**, the changes that we make depend on the time. Look at this sentence:

> *On 4 June 2007, Ann said to Alan, **'I'm meeting Clive tomorrow.'***

On the same day, Alan could say:
> *Ann says (that) **she's meeting** Clive **tomorrow**.*
> OR *Ann said (that) **she was meeting** Clive **tomorrow**.*

A week later, Alan could say:
> *Ann said (that) **she was meeting** Clive **the following day**.*

We do not have to change the tense and time words such as **tomorrow** if the thing reported has not happened yet, or is still true.

5 We can also use indirect questions like this:
> *Did Neil ask you **if you were from Sweden**?*
> *Who asked you **where Penny lived**?*
> *Did they phone to say **when they would arrive**?*

6 When we do not need to mention the subject we can form **indirect questions** with a **question word** + **infinitive**. Compare:
> *Geoff asked me **where to sit**. (= where he should sit)*
> *Geoff asked me where his parents should sit.*
> *I'm not sure **what to do**. (= what I should do)*
> *I'm not sure what Janet should do.*
> *I explained **how to make** an omelette.*
> *I explained how top chefs made an omelette.*

Grammar in action

③ We often use **indirect speech** after a phrase like **Could you tell me...?** or **Do you know...?** to make questions more polite:

> *Where is the tourist office?*
> OR *Could you tell me where the tourist office is?*
> *I wonder whether you could tell me where the tourist office is?*
> OR *Do you know where the tourist office is?*

④ We can use **indirect questions** to give information:
> *First, I'll tell you a little about what our company does, then I'll show you where your desk is.*
> *This is John, who will tell you how the computers work and what your password is.*
> *Here's Chris, who's going to take you on a tour of the building and show you where everything is.*

B The report depends on the situation

Make two reports with *tell* according to the different situations.

Fiona said 'I've lost my credit card.'

0 Your report, on the same day: Fiona tells me she's lost her credit card. 0

0 Your report, weeks later: Fiona told me she'd lost her credit card. 0

Sally said, 'Phil's going to phone me tomorrow.'

1 Your report, the same afternoon: Sally says 1

2 Your report, the following week: Sally, you told 2

Nick said, 'I passed my driving test last week.'

3 Your report, the same day: Nick tells 3

4 Your report, several weeks later: Nick, you said 4

Ken said, 'I'm sorry, I can't see you and Kate this weekend.'

5 Your report, the same day: Ken tells 5

6 Your report, weeks later: Ken told 6

C Summer course questions

At an introduction meeting at a language school, the director of studies answers students' questions. Use the students' notes to complete the exchanges between them and the director of studies.

> When is the trip to Stratford?
>
> Where can we buy course books?
>
> Does the school have an internet connection?
>
> How many students are there in a group?
>
> How will we be placed in the different levels?
>
> What time do we finish in the afternoon?
>
> Can we get drinks in the school?
>
> How do I get to the town centre?
>
> Which dictionary should we buy?

0 I'd like to know _when the trip to Stratford is._
~ It's next Friday.

1 Can you tell us _____?
~ At the bookshop in the basement.

2 I'd like to ask _____.
~ No, but there is an internet café across the street.

3 Could you clarify _____?
~ 12 in general classes and 8 in conversation classes.

4 I'm not sure _____.
~ After this meeting you'll all take a level test.

5 I'd like to know _____.
~ At half past four.

6 I'd like to ask _____.
~ Yes, there is a machine near the entrance.

7 Can you tell me _____.
~ Take the bus from the High Street.

8 We're not sure _____.
~ You should buy a good learner's dictionary.

WORD FOCUS

To clarify something means 'to make something clearer or easier to undertand'.

OVER TO YOU Now go to page 124.

15 Conditional sentences
Zero conditional and first conditional

1 A **conditional sentence** has two clauses: an **'if clause'** (e.g. **if the weather is fine**) and a **'result clause'** (e.g. **we eat in the garden**).

> *If the weather is fine, we eat in the garden.*
> *We'll go out if the weather is good tomorrow.*

Either clause or both clauses can be negative:

> *If the weather isn't fine, our dog doesn't like to go out.*
> *I'll be sad if the weather isn't good tomorrow.*

> **TIP**
> The **if clause** or the **result clause** can come first. We use a comma when the **if clause** comes first.

2 Zero conditional
We form **zero conditional** sentences with the verb in the **present simple** in **both clauses**:

> *Children **learn** quickly if they **are** interested.*
> *If you **have** a big car, you **pay** a lot for petrol.*

We use **zero conditionals** to talk about things that always happen, or things that happen in the same way every time:

> *If I **eat** too much, I **get** stomach ache.*
> *Felix's always in a good mood if his team **wins**.*

3 First conditional
We form **first conditional sentences** with the verb in the **present simple** in the **if clause**, and **will + verb** in the **result clause**:

> *If I **win** our tennis match, Dan **will be** very annoyed.*

We use the **first conditional** to talk about a future possibility when we feel confident about our predictions:

> *If they **don't leave** right now, they'**ll miss** the train.*

The **result clause** can have **going to**, **must**, **should** or an imperative instead of **will**:

> *There's **going to be** trouble if the neighbours **have** another all-night party.*
> *If you **have** a headache, you **should take** an aspirin.*

> **TIP**
> We can use **unless** to mean **if … not** e.g.:
> *They'll miss the train **unless** they leave right now.* (= if they don't leave …)
>
> A clause with **unless** usually comes second.

Grammar in action

1 We can use **zero conditionals** to give facts – this can be about science or rules in sport:
> *If you heat water to 100°C, it boils.* (scientific fact)
> *If he kicks a drop goal, his team gets 3 points.* (rules of rugby)

2 We use **zero conditionals** to talk about the behaviour of people we know, when they react in the same way every time:
> *If I get home late, my wife gets angry.*

3 We use the **first conditional** to talk about things that are possible in the future. This might be in a warning:
> *If you don't apologize, Keith will be very cross.*
> *If you don't get up now, you'll miss the bus.*

4 We also use the **first conditional** to make realistic predictions about our lives in the future:
> *If I fail my exams, I won't get into university.*

A What happens?

Match these phrases to make zero conditional sentences.

0	You have to pay a fine		**a**	if she eats seafood.
1	If I'm late for work,		**b**	the police come automatically.
2	Jane gets very ill		**c**	if his opponent misses the ball.
3	If water cools to 0°C,		**d**	if you get caught speeding.
4	He scores a point		**e**	my manager always notices.
5	If the alarm goes off,		**f**	it freezes.

B Father and son

Use the words given to make first conditional sentences including *if* and *will* and any necessary changes.

0 you / not / brush / your teeth / they / go / bad

If you don't brush your teeth, they'll go bad.

1 you / eat / all your vegetables / I / give / you some dessert

....

2 you / have / stomach ache / you / eat / too many plums

....

3 I / help / you with your homework / you / do / the washing-up?

....

4 you / not / go to bed now / you / be / tired in the morning

....

5 your mother / be / cross / you / come home late

....

C Change your behaviour

Re-write these sentences about changes of behaviour using *unless* and making any necessary changes.

0 If I don't lose weight, I'll have to buy new clothes.

I'll *have to buy new clothes unless I lose weight.*

1 If you stop buying CDs, you'll be able to afford a holiday.

You ....

2 If her cold isn't better, she won't go to school tomorrow.

She ....

3 If she studies hard, she'll pass the exam.

Unless ....

4 If you don't listen, you won't know what to do.

Unless ....

D Family finances

Complete this family discussion by using first conditionals with the words in brackets.

MUM We've got problems and if we ....*don't change*....0 (not, change), things
..........*will get*..........0 (get) worse.

DAD And we definitely ....1 (not, be) able to have a holiday if we
...........................2 (not, save) some money every month.

DELLA With petrol so expensive, if you two ....3 (stop) using two cars,
you ....4 (save) a lot of money.

ALEX And you ....5 (not, need) any bus money if you
...........................6 (go) to school on your bike.

DELLA I ....7 (not, be) able to use it unless someone
...........................8 (mend) the puncture.

ALEX Perhaps I should get a Saturday job. I ....9 (not, need) any
pocket money if I ....10 (earn) some of my own.

4 Second conditional
We form **second conditionals** with a past tense verb in the **if clause** and **would + verb** in the **result clause**:
*If Jane **was** here, she **would help** us.*
*The world **would be** boring if there **were** no animals.*
*What **would** you **do** if you **won** a lot of money?*
*If I **didn't live** in Scotland, I**'d want** to live in Germany.*

5 Notice that in the **if clause**, we can use **were** with **I** and with **he/she/it**:
*If **Jane were/was** here, she **would** certainly help us.*
*If I **were/was** French, I'd live in Paris.*

There is one expression where we always use **were**:
*If I **were you**, I'd tell him.* (NOT ~~If I was you, …~~)

6 Notice that we can use **could + infinitive** in both clauses:
*If you **could meet** a famous person, who would it be?*
*If the weather was fine, we **could go** to the zoo.*

7 Although the **second conditional** has a verb in the past tense, it does not refer to past time. We can use it to talk about the present when we imagine something different from the real situation now:
*If the sun **was** cold, life on earth **would be** impossible.*
*I'm not rich, but if I **was** rich, **would** I **be** happier?*

8 We can also use the **second conditional** to talk about situations that are unlikely in the future:
*The world **would be** a better place if there **were** no more wars.*

*Tom says that if he **won** the lottery, he **would give** all the money to poor people.*

> Notice that we can use both **first** and **second conditionals** to talk about the future:
> *If Sara passes her exam tomorrow, I'll be very pleased.* (first conditional; likely)
> *If Sara passed her exam tomorrow, I'd be very pleased.* (second conditional; unlikely)

Grammar in action

⑤ We can use the **second conditional** to imagine situations that are not true or unlikely:
What would you do if you were really well off, if you were a billionaire, for example? ~ Well, I'd stop working for a start. ~ Wouldn't you be bored if you had nothing to do? ~ If I stopped work, that wouldn't mean I'd have nothing to do, but I wouldn't have any fixed hours and I'd have lots of time for my favourite hobbies.

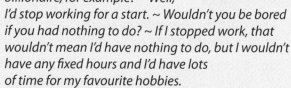

⑥ The **second conditional** is sometimes more polite than the first conditional when we are talking about the future:
If you offered me the job, I would accept it.

E People imagine things that are not true

Make second conditional sentences using one expression from column A and one from column B, using the words in brackets and putting the verbs in the correct form.

A	B
If Jenny (live) in the country	he (not, get) stomach ache.
You (enjoy) France more	I (tell) him the truth.
If I (be) you	if people (not fly) so much.
If my father (eat) more slowly	if you (can) speak better French.
There (be) less pollution	she (have) two or three dogs.

0 *If Jenny lived in the country, she would have two or three dogs.*

1 ....

2 ....

3 ....

4 ....

F Probable or unlikely?

Look at these first conditional sentences. Do they refer to a probable future event, or an unlikely situation? If they refer to an unlikely situation, change them to second conditional sentences.

0 If I win the lottery, I'll stop working and buy a yacht.

If I won the lottery, I would stop working and buy a yacht.

0 I'll put some petrol in the car if I go out this afternoon.

probable future event

1 Suzie will live in Beverly Hills if she can live anywhere in the world.

....

2 If I get home from work early, I'll take the dog for a walk.

....

3 If James rings, I'll tell him you're not here.

....

4 If the Queen rings, I'll be too shocked to speak.

....

5 If I have a million pounds, I'll buy a sports car.

....

6 If it rains tomorrow, I'll take an umbrella.

....

G Time for a change of job?

Complete the conversation by crossing out the wrong alternative in each case.

GWEN   I hate my work. If I I *have / had* [0] a better job, I *would be / was* [1] so much happier.

GARY   You need more qualifications: if you *had / have* [2] another qualification, you *can / could* [3] get something better. If you *have / had* [4] a perfectly free choice, what would you choose?

GWEN   Hmm, if I *could / can* [5] choose anything, I think *I'll / I'd* [6] want to be an actress.

GARY   And if that *is / was* [7] impossible, what *would / will* [8] your next choice be?

GWEN   Oh, I don't know. What *do / would* [9] you do if you *were / was* [10] me?

GARY   If I *was / were* [11] you, *I'll / I'd* [12] stop thinking about acting for a start. I'd choose something more realistic, like managing a shop. *I'd / I'll* [13] be confident to manage a sales team if I *can / could* [14] deal with people the way you do.

GWEN   But I don't know much about business.

GARY   Exactly, but if you *go / went* [15] to night school and *take / took* [16] a business course, in a year's time you'll have a diploma. I know a couple of people who've done that. If you like, I'll introduce you to them.

GWEN   I suppose I'll have a better idea if I *talk / talked* [17] to them.

GARY   Of course, if you do a course like that, *you'll / you'd* [18] have to work as well and you *won't / wouldn't* [19] have much spare time.

GWEN   True, but if *it's / it will be* [20] only for a year, I can manage that. What's certain is that if I *don't / won't* [21] make a move soon, it'll be too late because I'll lose my nerve.

GARY   Exactly! If you *think / thought* [22] about it too long, you won't do it.

OVER TO YOU Now go to page 124.

1 Look at the nouns in these sentences about a band:

> *Their **music** is very moving. Five of the **songs** made me cry.*

Music is an **uncountable noun**: it is something we cannot count or number, and it does not have a plural form. **Songs** is a **countable noun**: we can talk about 3, 4, 5 songs, etc., and it has both singular and plural forms (**song, songs**).

2 A/an; many/some; the + countable nouns
We use **a/an** with singular countable nouns when we do not need to make clear which person or thing we are talking about; we use **many/some/any/no** with plural countable nouns in the same way:

> *Jane entered **a salad** and **some brownies** in the school food competition.*
> *Were there **many people** at the party?*
> *There aren't **any eggs** / are **no eggs** in the cupboard.*

When people can understand which person or thing we mean, we use **the** with singular and plural countable nouns:

> *The salad won a prize but **the judges** didn't like **the brownies**.*

3 Much/some; the + uncountable nouns
We use **much/some/any/no** with uncountable nouns:

> *There isn't **much snow** this year.*
> *Could I have **some water**, please?*
> *There isn't **any butter** / is **no butter** in the fridge.*

When people know what we are referring to, we can use **the** with uncountable nouns:

> *Did you enjoy the meal? ~ Yes, I liked **the food**.*
> *(= the food in the meal)*

4 No article
We use no article with plural countable nouns and with uncountable nouns when we are talking in general:

> ***Dogs** don't usually like **cats**.*
> ***Water** is a compound of **hydrogen** and **oxygen**.*
> ***Good health** is more important than **money**.*

5 Some nouns can be countable or uncountable, with different meanings:

> *Would you like **a glass** of water?*
> *Our new coffee table has a top made of **glass**.*

> *I've seen that film three **times**.*
> *Now we don't have enough **time** to relax.*

> *She quit her job to start **a business** selling ice cream.*
> ***Business** is booming.*

Grammar in action

1 The nouns for many types of food are **uncountable**, particularly drinks (e.g. **coffee, tea, beer, water**), foods derived from milk or grains (e.g. **butter, cheese, pasta, rice, sugar, salt, flour**), and meat and fish when we do not mean the whole animal (e.g. **beef, tuna**):

> *We ate beef with rice, and drank mineral water.*

We often talk about containers (e.g. **a glass, a bowl, a jar, a packet**) and quantities (e.g. 500g) of these things, with **of**:

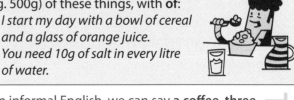

> *I start my day with a bowl of cereal and a glass of orange juice.*
> *You need 10g of salt in every litre of water.*

2 Many abstract feelings, ideas, and the names of subjects of study are **uncountable**, e.g. **love, happiness, joy, sorrow, philosophy, economics**:

> *If you're interested in the economics of happiness, there's an article about it in this month's Journal.*

3 When we discuss a subject in general, we use **uncountable nouns** and **plural countable nouns** with no article:

> *Humans need a balanced diet. We need protein in the form of meat or fish and we need carbohydrates like bread and pasta. We also need vegetables and fruit. And of course we cannot live without liquids, which basically means water.*

A Holiday conversation

Complete the dialogue by writing *a*, *an*, or *the* in the gaps, or - if no article is necessary.

LEO   Hello, Lucy. You're brown. Do you use ....—........ [0] fake tan cream or have you been in ....*the*.... [0] sun?

LUCY   It's a real tan. .... [1] friend and I have just come back from the Algarve.

LEO   I've never been to .... [2] south of Portugal. Did you stay on .... [3] coast?

LUCY   Yes, we stayed in .... [4] small hotel in .... [5] little fishing village. .... [6] hotel had .... [7] small rooms but .... [8] large open terrace where we had our meals.

LEO   Did they serve .... [9] good food?

LUCY   Yes, on the whole .... [10] food was fine. We had .... [11] fresh fish almost every evening. And we had lots of .... [12] fruit. .... [13] peaches were wonderful.

LEO   Was there no danger from .... [14] bugs?

LUCY   No, ... [15] hotel owner told us that they always washed .... [16] fruit in .... [17] water before serving it.

LEO   It all sounds very nice. I hope you'll let me see .... [18] photos you took.

B Study and work

Complete the text by choosing between the options and by using the words in the box, making them plural if necessary.

| accommodation hope information philosophy result time trip university |

When I finished school, I applied to study *the*/- ...*philosophy*... [0] at two ...*universities*... [0], Sheffield (my home town) and London. I didn't have *much/many* [1] .... [2] of getting into London University because my school exam .... [3] were not brilliant. But I was lucky and I was accepted there. I had to make two .... [4] to London before I started, one for the interview and another to find .... [5]. The university provided students with *an/some* [6] .... [7] about flats and it didn't take very *many/much* [8] .... [9] to find a room.

| chance experience job languages money work |

While I was studying, I didn't think about .... [10] – I mean, how I would earn my living after university. (My parents said that I had never been particularly worried about *the*/- [11] .... [12].) When the time came, I realized that *the*/- [13] .... [14] had always interested me so I applied for several .... [15] teaching English abroad. Obviously, I didn't have *an/any* [16] .... [17] but I thought I had a small .... [18] of being accepted.

| job luck news time weather |

In the end, a letter came and I felt nervous as I opened it. But the .... [19] *was/were* [20] good! The letter offered me *a*/- [21] work in a Swedish school. I knew the winter .... [22] in Sweden *was/were* [23] cold so I bought some warm clothes. Then I had *a/some* [24] farewell party and everyone wished me good .... [25] in my new life as a teacher. Since then I have had a lot of .... [26] in different countries and I am happy to say that I have enjoyed all of them. But I have wondered *many/much* [27] .... [28] what would have happened if that first letter had turned me down.

16 Nouns
Noun + noun

6 We can often put one noun before another, e.g.:
    *a **gold watch*** (= a watch made of gold)
    *two **milk bottles*** (= bottles for holding milk)
    *a **flower shop*** (= a shop that sells flowers)
    *a **furniture van*** (= a van that carries furniture)

The first noun can be an *-ing* form, e.g.: **swimming** pool, **reading** lamp, **dancing** shoes, **dining** room

Sometimes the two nouns are written as one word. Here are some examples:

> airline   bedroom   bookshelf   boyfriend
> desktop   dishwasher   earring   girlfriend
> haircut   hairdryer   headache   headphones
> newspaper   policeman   postman
> sightseeing   teacup   toothpaste

Sometimes we use a hyphen (-), e.g.: **baby-sitter**, **coffee-pot**.

Grammar in action

4 We often use a **noun + noun structure** to refer to the material something is made from. The second noun refers to the object, the first noun refers to the material:
    *I got a **silver ring** and a **glass vase** for my birthday.*
    (= a ring made of silver; a vase made of glass)

5 We can use a **noun + noun structure** to talk about an object's purpose: the first noun refers to what the second noun is for.
    *We should put the **reading lamp** on top of the **bookshelf.***
    (= a lamp for reading; a shelf for books)

6 We can use a **noun + noun structure** to say what a book, film, etc. is about:
    *There's a new **war film** on at the Odeon cinema.*
    *I've lost my **chemistry book**.*

7 We can use a **noun + noun structure** to talk about a person or machine that does an action. The second noun is made from a verb + **-er**:
    *Jim's training to be a **taxi driver**.*
    (= someone who drives a taxi)
    *Did you pack your **hairdryer**?*
    (= something that dries hair)

8 Notice the difference between the way we talk about empty and full containers:

container	container with contents
a milk bottle	a bottle of milk
two beer cans	two cans of beer
a coffee cup	a cup of coffee

> **TIP**
>
> Notice that the first noun is usually singular even when the meaning is plural, e.g.:
>   *a **flower** shop* (= a shop that sells flowers)
>   *a **dish**washer* (= a machine that washes dishes)
>
> Some common exceptions are:
>   *a **clothes** shop; a **sports** car; a **glasses** case*
>   (= a case for (reading) glasses)

C   Things you find in a house

Complete the sentences with a noun + noun structure.

0 A container for drinking tea is a ....*teacup*........ .

1 You can decorate walls with paper called ....

2 A .... is a kind of stereo that plays CDs.

3 You use a .... to file your nails.

4 The door into the kitchen is the ....

5 Put your dirty clothes in the .... and turn it on.

6 A bowl for fruit is a ....

7 A .... is for cutting bread.

8 Gloves made of rubber are ....

D   The container alone, or the container and the contents?

In these sentences cross out the wrong expression.

0   Who's going to take the ~~bottles of water~~ / water bottles to the recycling centre?
1   Would you like a *cup of coffee* / *coffee cup*?
2   Yesterday I bought two *packets of crisps* / *crisp packets*.
3   Tea tastes better in a proper *cup of tea* / *teacup*.
4   *Cans of cola* / *Cola cans* are very light.
5   I took the spider home in a *box of matches* / *matchbox* that I found.
6   There isn't much food but we have a couple of *cans of soup* / *soup cans*.
7   I keep old coins in a *jar of jam* / *jam jar*.
8   I've made some fresh tea in the blue *pot of tea* / *teapot*.

E   Out shopping

Complete the text about a shopping trip by filling each blank with one word from the box and the word in brackets, making any necessary changes.

bag	bar	card	centre	friend	girl	juice	market	pie
shoe	shopping	sports	stall	stop	summer	tennis	walk	

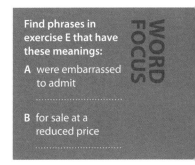

WORD FOCUS

Find phrases in exercise E that have these meanings:

A were embarrassed to admit

....

B for sale at a reduced price

....

Last Saturday I went shopping. I don't like all those ___plastic bags___ ⁰ (plastic) they give you so I always take my ___shopping bag___ ⁰ (bag). At the _____¹ (bus) I met an old _____² (school) called Katie. I hadn't seen her since we were at _____³ (camp) together about eight years ago. We talked about the camp and the _____⁴ (teachers). We both confessed that we fell in love with the _____⁵ (coach) although his _____⁶ (friend) was at the camp as well. When the bus got to the _____⁷ (town), we agreed to meet at a _____⁸ (coffee) after we'd finished shopping. First, I went to my favourite _____⁹ (shop) and bought a pair of _____¹⁰ (shoes) because next weekend I'm going to Scotland. Then I walked along the _____¹¹ (street). I stopped at a _____¹² (fruit) and bought some oranges and apples. They don't accept _____¹³ (credit) so I had to pay in cash. Next, I went to the supermarket and got the groceries, including an _____¹⁴ (apple) because they were on offer. Then I met Katie again and we talked for an hour while we enjoyed two glasses of _____¹⁵ (orange).

OVER TO YOU   Now go to page 124.

17 Possessives
Possessive adjectives and pronouns

1 The **possessive adjectives** are **my, your, his, her, its, our, your, their.**

*I hear **your** brother is in love with **my** sister.*
*Has Ellen phoned **her** mother?*
*What's **your** phone number? ~ **Our** home number is 935 441 635.*

We can use **your**, like **you**, to talk to one or more people:

*Everyone, put away **your** sweets and Jim, take out **your** book.*

Note that these adjectives have only one form:

***your** book   **your** books* (NOT ~~yours books~~)

2 The **possessive pronouns** are **mine, yours, his, hers, ours, yours, theirs,** and the possessive question word is **whose:**

*Is this Jane's bag? ~ No, this one is **mine**; that one is **hers**.*
*Their flat is bigger than **ours**.*
***Whose** book is this? / **Whose** is this book?*

(There is no pronoun corresponding to possessive adjective **it**.)

3 We use **possessive pronouns** when we do not need to repeat a noun:

*Most people like their name but I don't like **mine**.* (= my name)
*Our phone number is 935 441 635. What's **yours**?* (= your phone number)
*Tony and Helen both have dark hair but **his** is curly and **hers** is straight.* (= his hair and her hair)

> **TIP**
> Notice the difference between pronoun **its** and **it's** (the short form of **it is**), e.g.:
> *I saw the car but I didn't get **its** number.*
> *Whose is that car? ~ **It's** Peggy's.*

Grammar in action

1 We can use **possessive adjectives** and **pronouns** to talk about things we own:

My new mobile's an LG Prada. What make is yours? ~ Mine's a Sony, like my MP3 player.

2 We can use **possessive adjectives** and **pronouns** to talk about relationships with family, friends, and colleagues:

My dad's stronger than yours.
His manager is very helpful – mine isn't.

3 We use **possessive adjectives** and **pronouns** to talk about parts of the body:

Jeff has hurt his hand. (NOT ~~the hand~~)
Bend down and touch your toes. (NOT ~~the toes~~)
~ Anna can touch hers, but I can't touch mine.

4 We can use **possessive adjectives** and **pronouns** to talk about thoughts, feelings, ideas, etc. that we have:

When you told Molly she was fat, you really hurt her feelings.
It wasn't my idea to get the bus – it was yours.

> **TIP**
> We often use possessive adjectives with **left** and **right** with the meaning **to the left of me/you** etc.:
> *He's on my left.*

A   My family

Use possessive adjectives to complete this dialogue.

LIAM   Have I shown you these photos of ......*my*......⁰ family?

ANNA   No, you haven't. I've never seen any photos of ....¹ family.

LIAM   Look at this one. Here you can see me in the middle and on ....²
left is ....³ brother, Richard.

ANNA   Is ....⁴ brother older than you?

LIAM   Yes, he's 32. Next to him is .... [5] wife. .... [6] name is Sarah and she's holding .... [7] new baby. On the left of the picture is Tilly and .... [8] husband, Dave.

ANNA   Ah, yes, I've met Dave. .... [9] family lives in Australia.

LIAM   .... [10] grandparents - my dad's parents - are sitting at the front. Richard and Sarah's older children are sitting on .... [11] knees.

ANNA   And where are .... [12] parents?

LIAM   Mum and Dad are in this other photo here, look …

B Sharing

Possessive pronoun or possessive adjective? Choose the appropriate words to complete the story.

When I was a kid, *my / mine* [0] sister and I always got the same presents. We both got a dress, for example, but *mine / my* [1] was green and *hers / her* [2] was pink. One year, *ours / our* [3] parents got us kites, but they were exactly the same. There was no way to know whose was whose. One day, I was playing with *my / mine* [4] in the garden, and I broke it, just a little bit. I didn't tell anyone, but I went to *my / mine* [5] sister's room and swapped it for *her / hers* [6]. The next day, *our / ours* [7] family went to the beach. There were some other children there and they loved *our / ours* [8] kites. *Mine / My* [9] sister saw the kids and said, 'They haven't got a kite, I'm going to give them *my / mine* [10].' I felt terrible. *Mine / My* [11] sister has always been nicer than me!

C Hobbies

Complete this dialogue by putting a possessive adjective, a possessive pronoun, *who*, *whose*, *it's* or *its* in each gap.

ZOË   What's ___your___ [0] favourite hobby?

ZAC   Swimming. What's .... [1]?

ZOË   My sister and I are into skateboarding. We've just got new boards. I bought a British one but .... [2] is American.

ZAC   .... [3] is best?

ZOË   I think .... [4] is, of course! Grace got an American one because she says .... [5] wheels are stronger, but .... [6] board doesn't feel very different from mine. And I think .... [7] a horrible colour too!

ZAC   Isn't skateboarding dangerous? .... [8] mum won't let me try it.

ZOË   Not if you're careful like me, but Grace broke .... [9] arm last year.

ZAC   And do you go in for competitions?

ZOË   Yeah, we do these team events. .... [10] team came third the last time we entered. .... [11] exciting to skate against other people.

ZAC   Perhaps you'll do even better with .... [12] new boards.

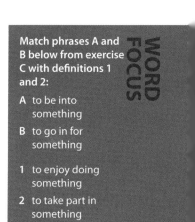

WORD FOCUS

Match phrases A and B below from exercise C with definitions 1 and 2:

A to be into something

B to go in for something

1 to enjoy doing something

2 to take part in something

Possessives
's and s'; of mine

4 We make the **possessive form** of singular nouns by adding **'s**:

> Sally – **Sally's** cousin   Charles – **Charles's** friend
> my mum – my **mum's** coat
> the boss – the **boss's** office

5 We make the **possessive form** of regular plural nouns by adding an apostrophe (') to the plural form:

> girls – the **girls'** changing rooms
> workers – **workers'** rights
> parents – my **parents'** wedding photos

6 We make the **possessive form** of irregular plural nouns by adding **'s**:

> women – **women's** shoes
> children – our **children's** toys
> people – most **people's** ideas

7 We can use **noun** + **'s** or **s'** without a following noun, when the thing we are talking about has just been mentioned:

> Whose is this bike? ~ It's **Clive's**.
> I can see the **ladies'** toilet but where's the **men's**?

8 We can sometimes use a phrase with **of**, normally when we are talking about **things**, not people or animals:

> They've painted the **side of their house** blue.
> I'm studying the **history of philosophy**.
> The **smell of** freshly baked **bread** is delicious.

9 We can also form **double possessives** like this:

> a cousin of Sally's
> (= one of Sally's cousins; NOT ~~a cousin of Sally~~)
> some friends of mine
> (= some of my friends; NOT ~~some friends of me~~)

> You will sometimes see names ending in **s** without the addition of **'s**, to avoid the double s sound:
> Charles – **Charles'** friend OR **Charles's** friend
> St. James – St. **James'** Street OR St **James's** Street

TIP

Grammar in action

5 We can use **noun** + **'s** or **s'** and structures with **of** to talk about things we own; to talk about our relationships with family, friends and colleagues; to talk about parts of the body; and to talk about ideas that we have:

> I really like Helen's new hairstyle.
> They're redecorating Paul's house at the moment.
> My cousin's birthday party is next Saturday.
> I thought Martin's suggestion was very helpful.

D   Exam results

Look at the exam results and complete the sentences using possessive forms.

	Olivia	Daniel	Joseph	Jessica	Ben	Sophie
History	79	57	63	74	71	72
Art	54	69	83	67	74	68

0   Jessica / history result / better / Sophie
Jessica's history result was better than Sophie's.

1   Olivia / history result / better than / Jessica

2   Ben / history result / better than / Daniel / and / Joseph

3   In general, the / girls / history results / better than / boys

4   In art, though, the / boys / results / better than / girls

E Book titles

Look at these titles of English novels. Tick the correct title. Remember: we use 's for people, animals and businesses or institutions, and *of* for abstract ideas.

0 The *Aunt's Story* ___✓___ or *The Story of the Aunt* ___

1 *Innocence's Age* ___ or *The Age of Innocence* ___

2 *Giovanni's Room* ___ or *The Room of Giovanni* ___

3 *The Magician's Nephew* ___ or *The Nephew of the Magician* ___

4 *Schindler's Ark* ___ or *The Ark of Schindler* ___

5 *The Power's Corridors* ___ or *The Corridors of Power* ___

6 *The Horse's Mouth* ___ or *The Mouth of the Horse* ___

7 *Silence's Towers* ___ or *Towers of Silence* ___

8 *On Her Majesty's Secret Service* ___ or *On the Secret Service of Her Majesty* ___

F New gadgets

Complete the dialogue by using the word in brackets to make a possessive form.

ANNE Is that ___*your*___ [0] (you) new mobile?

JACK Yes, I got it from that shop where ___ [1] (Harry) mother works. It's the same model as my ___ [2] (sister), although ___ [3] (she) is black.

ANNE I bet it can do lots of things that ___ [4] (I) can't.

JACK ___ [5] (You) is pretty old, isn't it?

ANNE Yes, it's almost three years old. It used to be my ___ [6] (brother) but he gave it to me when ___ [7] (he) company gave him one of ___ [8] (they).

JACK Well, ___ [9] (I) new one can record videos.

ANNE That's like my ___ [10] (parents) new digital camera.

JACK Yes, every new model has to be better than the last.

ANNE Do you think ___ [11] (we) lives are better for all these changes?

JACK Not really, and I suppose the generations after ___ [12] (we) will wonder why companies didn't make some real progress instead of bringing out new gadgets every year.

ANNE At least you can recycle ___ [13] (you) old phone, or give it to charity. A cousin of ___ [14] (Melanie) works for an organization that sends phones to Africa. ___ [15] (It) work also involves donating money to some of the poorest communities.

JACK That's great. Hey, can you give me ___ [16] (they) details and I'll send them ___ [17] (I) old phone.

OVER TO YOU Now go to page 124.

1 The **demonstrative adjectives** are **this**, **that**, **these** and **those**:
> Can you take **this letter** to the bank, please?
> Go and stand by **that tree** over there.
> **These rings** belonged to my grandmother.
> What are **those girls** looking at?

2 We use **this** and **that** with singular nouns and uncountable nouns. We use **these** and **those** with plural nouns.

We can also use them without nouns when the meaning is clear:
> **That's** Paul's bike and **this** is mine. (*That* = That bike; *this* = this bike)

(For more examples of this use see p. 72.)

3 We use **this** and **these** for things that are near to us:
> I think **this money** belongs to Harry.
> **These clothes** are really dirty!

We use **that** and **those** for things that are not near to us:
> Go and stand by **that tree** over there.
> **Those boys** are waving at you!

4 We use **this** and **these** to talk about things that are near in time (= happening now or just going to happen):
> I like listening to **this programme**.
> (= the programme on the radio now)
> I love **these** long **summer evenings**.
> (= It is summer now.)

We often use **this** in time phrases such as **this week**, **this month**, **this season**, **this year**, etc. when we are talking about the period of time around now:
> There has been a lot of rain **this month**.
> Are you working every day **this week**?

We use **that** and **those** for things that are further away in time (= just finished or in the past):
> **That dinner** we had last night was wonderful. (= in the past)
> Do you remember **those camping trips** we went on with Grandad? (= in the past)

> **TIP**
>
> When we do not need to repeat a singular noun, we tend to use **this one** and **that one**, not **this** and **that**, e.g.:
> > Which tie do you prefer? ~ I like **this one** best.
> > These cars are French but **that one's** German.
>
> When we include an adjective, we use **one(s)** instead of repeating the noun, e.g.:
> > I don't like this dress but I like **that blue one**. (NOT … I like ~~that blue~~.)
> > I used to like pop songs but I don't like **these new ones**. (NOT … ~~these new~~.)

Grammar in action

1 We use **this** and **these** to talk about our activities in the present or future:
> Have you tried **these cakes**?
> I'm really enjoying **this party**.

We use **that** and **those** to talk about activities in the past. Here, we're talking about a trip last week:
> What's the name of **those yellow fish** that we saw at the zoo?
> **That elephant** obviously liked apples!

2 On a journey we use **this** for places we are going to arrive in, and **that** for places we have passed:
> What's the name of **that castle** that we saw a few minutes ago?
> **This next village** is called Bakewell.

A   Then and now

Complete these short exchanges with *this, that, these* or *those*.

Last weekend we visited ....*that*....⁰ country house near Nottingham.

~ Are the opening hours ....¹ year the same as last year?

Do you remember ....² parties we had before we got married?

~ Yes. Don't say anything to Debbie but I don't like ....³ one at all. I wish we had stayed at home tonight.

.... ⁴ goal in the first half was fantastic, but .... ⁵ second half is disappointing.
~ I agree. I'll be glad when it's all over.

I read in .... ⁶ morning's newspaper that long skirts are coming back.
~ Thank goodness. I don't like the short skirts that everybody's wearing .... ⁷ days.

I was just thinking about .... ⁸ dreadful package holidays we used to go on with Jake and Debbie.
~ Ugh! Don't remind me! Thank goodness they've already booked a cruise for .... ⁹ summer – we can go somewhere nice!

WORD FOCUS

Find words from exercise A that have these meanings:

A not as good as expected

....

B terrible

B Which one do you prefer?

Complete the sentences with *this*, *that*, *these*, *those*, *one* or *ones*.

1 Do you prefer ..this.. striped blouse or flowery .... ?

2 I'm not sure whether I prefer .... smart shoes or .... casual ....

3 Which do you prefer? .... strong Swiss cheese or milder French .... ?

4 Well, my dear, do you prefer .... tall lamp or .... short .... ?

5 I'm not sure whether I like .... round sunglasses or .... square ....

6 I like .... long skirt, but I also like .... short ....

5 Here are some more examples of **this**, **that**, **these** and **those** without a noun. We use this structure when the meaning is clear without using a noun:

> *These are my favourite chocolates!* (These = these chocolates)
> *This painting is OK, but I prefer **those** over there.*

Or when we want to point to something that is about to happen, or something that happened in the past:

> *This is very interesting.* (*This* = the thing I am going to say now)
> *What was **that**?* (*that* = the sound that we have just heard)

Grammar in action

3 We use **this** to point to something we are going to do next. We want to draw someone's attention to what is about to happen. This is very common in informal situations, such as showing our friends or family our skills:

> *Hey Mum! I can do a jump on my bike! Watch this!* (= the thing I am about to do)

And we use **that** to point to something that has just happened. In this example, Mum has just seen the jump:

> *Well done, Charlie! That was amazing!* (= the jump)

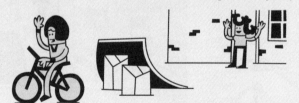

4 In more formal situations, we can use **this** and **these** to point to the thing we are going to say next. We want to emphasize that our next sentence contains important information. This might be when we are speaking to colleagues at work:

> *This is what Jack said: either we start the project now or we'll have to wait till next month.* (= The thing I am going to say next is Jack's suggestion.)
> *The two main points are these: we must work together and everything must be ready by Friday.* (= The things I am going to say next are the main points.)

And we use **that** and **those** to point to things that we have already said. We want to refer to information that has been said before:

> *The hospital needs to be expanded, but I'm not here to talk about that.* (= the topic I have just mentioned)

5 We can use **this is** on the telephone to say who is speaking:

> *Hello, this is Derek Mills. I'm phoning about my hotel reservation.*

When phoning friends and family we might just use **it's**. **It's** is less formal than **this is**. Contrast:

> *Hello, Mrs. Bell, **this is** Amir. Is Peter at home?*
> *Hi, Dad, **it's** Melissa!*

We can also use **it's … here**. This can be used in formal situations, too:

> *Hello, it's Professor Chambers here, I'm calling about the conference.*

We would not say **this is … here**.

6 We can use **this is** to introduce people:

> *Matthew, this is my sister, Abigail. And this is her husband, Mitesh.*

C   Things to come; things from a moment before; introductions

Complete the mini-dialogues with *this*, *that*, *this is* and *that's*.

Listen to ....*this*........ ⁰! What's brown and sticky? … A brown stick! Ha ha ha!
~ Aargh! .... ¹ a really old joke.

And look, ... ² the best bit, he actually falls off the wall!
~ OK! .... ³ enough! I can't watch any more of .... ⁴.

Hi, Jane, ... [5] Marion, I'm just phoning to say congratulations on your new job!
~ Oh, thanks, ... [6] very kind.

Look at .... [7]. I bought it at the auction on Saturday.
~ Wow! .... [8] amazing! It must have cost a fortune.

.... [9] is the 10 o'clock news: two soldiers have been awarded …
~ … and .... [10] was the latest news bulletin with Fiona Bruce …

D Making a speech

Complete these extracts from speeches by circling the correct option.

A

Ladies and gentlemen, I am pleased to be at *(this)/that* [0] meeting today. It is not my job to make a long speech, but I would like to begin the meeting by telling you *this/that* [1] true story. Several years ago, I had a serious illness. At *this/that* [2] time, medicine was not as advanced as it is *these/those* [3] days …

B

… I enjoyed my time at university. *These/Those* [4] were the best years of my life. Then I was in the army for two years. After *this/that* [5], I moved to Glasgow to work in a research institute. *This/That* [6] was where I met my wife. I know she's watching *this/that* [7] on the TV at home and I would just like to send her *these/those* [8] words: without you I wouldn't be here today.

E Two brothers

Matt asks his younger brother to help him. Complete the dialogue by putting in *this, that, these,* or *those.*

MATT   Tim! What are you doing?
TIM   I'm just doing ....this.... [0] crossword. It's a bit difficult.
MATT   Well, if you help me with something now, I'll help you with .... [1] later.
TIM   I've heard .... [2] before!
MATT   OK, but I'm serious .... [3] time. Listen. .... [4] is what I want you to do. Here, take .... [5] photos. I want you to take them to Sylvia.
TIM   Why can't you go yourself?
MATT   I've got .... [6] terrible cold and I'd rather stay at home.
TIM   You didn't have a cold .... [7] morning.
MATT   Well, it doesn't matter. Listen. Sylvia lives in one of .... [8] houses on the other side of the park.
TIM   .... [9] is a posh area. I can't go there dressed like .... [10]. .... [11] jeans have got holes in them.
MATT   Well, put .... [12] new ones on – the ones you bought last Saturday. Anyway, Sylvia lives at number 13. Just give her the photos and tell her that I'll see her .... [13] weekend.
TIM   OK, but you owe me for .... [14]. I want more than just some help with .... [15] crossword.
MATT   OK, OK.

OVER TO YOU Now go to page 124.

19 Quantifiers
Some, any, no; much, many, a lot of

1 We use **some** and **any** before plural nouns or uncountable nouns when we do not need to give an exact quantity or amount:

> There were **some pens** on the desk but there wasn't **any paper**.

We can also use them without nouns when the meaning is clear:

> Hannah needed some paper but she couldn't find **any**. (any = any paper)

2 We use **some** in positive sentences:

> I bought **some** cola and Tim bought **some** sandwiches.

And we use **any** in negative sentences, and with words such as **never** or **without**, which have negative meanings:

> I **never** have **any** clean socks!
> I managed to use the washing machine **without any** problems.

3 We use **any** in questions when we do not know what answer to expect:

> Have you got **any** brothers or sisters?
> Do you have **any** photos of your dog?

However, we use **some** in questions when we expect the answer 'yes':

> Would you like **some** more cake?
> Could I have **some** tea, please?

4 We can use **no** instead of **not … any** with plural nouns or uncountable nouns. **No** is stronger than **not … any** and is often used in more formal situations:

> I **don't** have **any** time to speak to you now.
> I have **no** time to speak to you now.

We must use **no** with a noun, but we use **none** on its own to express the same meaning:

> I wanted to buy a ticket for the concert, but there were **none** left. (none = no tickets)

> We can use **some**, **any** and **none** + **of**:
> *some of the boys; any of the people; none of the teachers*

5 We use **a lot of**, **much** and **many** to talk about a large quantity of something. We use **much** with uncountable nouns, and **many** with plural nouns. **A lot of** goes with both uncountable and plural nouns:

> There are **a lot of flowers** but there isn't **much grass** or **many trees**.

6 We normally use **a lot of** in positive sentences and **much** and **many** in negative sentences and questions:

> Sarah **has a lot of books** at home.
> **Have** you **read many books** in French?
> Harry **doesn't have much time** to read.

7 We can use **(a) few** instead of **not many** and **(a) little** instead of **not much**:

> I've eaten **a few** strawberries with **a little** cream.

8 We can use **a lot of**, **much**, **many**, **(a) few** and **(a) little** without nouns when the meaning is clear:

> I didn't eat **much** at lunchtime, so I was hungry when we arrived! ~ Were there many people? ~ No, not **many**, just **a few**. (*much* = much food; *many* = many people; *a few* = a few people)

Grammar in action

1 We use **some**, **any**, **no**, **none**, etc. to talk about the amount or number of something when we don't have to be exact. This might be when we're deciding what to buy at the shops:

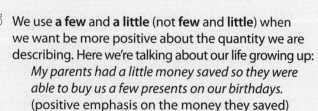

> Do we need any tomatoes? ~ There are a few left, but perhaps we should get some more. And there isn't much cheese, so we should buy some for the pizzas.

2 We use **some** in questions to make offers and requests:

> Can I have some extra time to finish my homework,?
> ~ Would you like some help with the last exercise?

3 We use **no** in formal signs when something is against the rules:

> No pets allowed in the restaurant.

4 We use **any** and **no** to make short sentences in everyday conversation:

> Any news? ~ Sorry, no time to stop and chat now!

5 We use **a few** and **a little** (not **few** and **little**) when we want be more positive about the quantity we are describing. Here we're talking about our life growing up:

> My parents had a little money saved so they were able to buy us a few presents on our birthdays. (positive emphasis on the money they saved)

Compare:

> My parents had little money so they bought us few presents and we couldn't afford to go on holiday. (more negative emphasis on the small amount of money.)

A What we need to buy

URGENT	OTHER
apples	pepper
sugar	bananas
biscuits	paper napkins
butter	olive oil
potatoes	vinegar

Four friends share a flat and put things on the shopping list. They put things under 'Urgent' when the item is finished and under 'Other' when the item is almost finished. Complete the statements using *any, no, a little* or *a few*.

0 There are ......*no*...... apples left, but they've still got ..*a little*.. pepper.

1 They've got .... bananas but they haven't got .... sugar.

2 There's .... butter and only .... olive oil.

3 They've got .... paper napkins but there are .... biscuits at all.

4 They've still got .... vinegar but they haven't got .... potatoes.

B   In a clothes shop

Complete these shop conversations by circling the right expression in each case.

ASSISTANT   Good morning. Can I help you?

MARK   Yes, I'd like to look at *some*/*any*⁰ shirts, please.

ASSISTANT   *Some/Any*¹ particular kind?

MARK   Plain ones, with *no/any*² pattern, or perhaps with just *a little/a few*³ decoration.

SAPNA   Have you got *some/any*⁴ smart skirts or trousers in the sale? I need them for work.

ASSISTANT   We've got *a little/a few*⁵ smart skirts in the sale but I'm afraid we haven't got *some/any*⁶ trousers. But there are *some/any*⁷ nice new trousers that have just come in and they aren't very expensive.

KIRSTEN   I'm looking for *some/any*⁸ shoes to go with this suit. I can't see *some/any*⁹ suitable ones in the window.

ASSISTANT   There isn't *much/many*¹⁰ room in the window so we only have *a little/a few*¹¹ pairs there. If you look at the back of the shop you'll find *much/a lot*¹² of styles to choose from.

FABIAN   Excuse me, are these socks all cotton?

ASSISTANT   Yes, they're all cotton. There's *any/no*¹³ other material in *some/any*¹⁴ of the socks on this shelf, but these over here have *a little/a few*¹⁵ lycra in them. Let's see. Yes, 90% cotton, 10% lycra. These days, *a lot of/much*¹⁶ socks have *a little/little*¹⁷ lycra in them.

19 Quantifiers
Pronouns: *somebody, everything*, etc.

9 With **some**, **any**, **no** and **every** we can form words ending in -**body**, -**one**, -**thing** and -**where**:

> *Did you hear **something**? I think I heard a knock, so perhaps there's **somebody** at the door. ~ I didn't hear **anything** and there's **no one** outside.*

Grammar in action

⑥ We use **somebody/someone** and **anybody/anyone** to refer to a person. We use these words in the same way as we use **some** and **any** (see p. 74):

> Positive: *We need someone who speaks Chinese.*
> Negative: *I haven't spoken to anybody about the fire.*
> Question: *Does anybody live in that house?*
> Offer/request: *Can I get you something to drink?*

Everybody/everyone is singular and refers to all the people in a group. We use these words before or after verbs:

> *We asked for volunteers and everybody was happy to help.*
> *I've invited everyone from work to come to the wedding but I haven't invited everyone I knew at school.*

We use **nobody / no one** (two words) in sentences with a positive verb to refer to people:

> *Nobody has replied to my invitation.*

⑦ We use **something**, **anything**, and **nothing** to refer to a thing or an idea. Here, we're asking for help from a friend:

> *I need to ask you a favour. Can you do something for me? ~ I'll do anything I can! I've got nothing to do this afternoon.*

Everything is singular and refers to all the items in a group of things or ideas:

> *Everything in this house belongs to me!*

⑧ We use **somewhere**, **anywhere**, **nowhere**, and **everywhere** to refer to places. Here, we're trying to find an item that is lost:

> *I can't find my bag anywhere and I've looked everywhere I can think of! ~ Now, don't be so dramatic. It must be somewhere! ~ No, really, it's nowhere to be seen.*

⑨ Notice that there is another use of **any**, **anybody**, **anyone**, **anything**, and **anywhere**. We use them in positive sentences to indicate that the choice is free or that everything is possible:

> *You can read any book from the top shelf.*
> (= You are free to choose which book you want.)
> *Anything would be more interesting than that new romance you've bought!*
> (= All the books would be better.)

C Quiz team

These are the five members of a team that is going to take part in a general knowledge quiz. Complete the questions and answers about the team using the words from the box.

	Profession	Hobbies/Interests
Sara	photographer	fashion, astrology
Mike	lawyer	gardening, foreign films
Lester	chef	skiing, snowboarding
Mary	chemist	theatre
Ron	astronomer	languages

something   nobody   everything   somebody   everything   ~~anybody~~
anybody   somewhere   something   anything   anybody   somebody
everything   everywhere   anybody   everything   everything

JANE   Have you got ....*anybody*........ ⁰ who knows about fashion?

FRANK   Yes, Sara reads all the magazines. She knows ....¹ about the latest styles.

JANE   You must have _____ ² who knows about the universe, they often ask about the planets.

FRANK   I think Ron knows _____ ³ about astronomy.

JANE   Is there _____ ⁴ who knows _____ ⁵ about cinema?

FRANK   Yes, Mike knows _____ ⁶ about it. He mostly watches European films though, I think.

JANE   Have you got _____ ⁷ who works in politics?

FRANK   No, we've got _____ ⁸ who actually works in politics. But Mike will know _____ ⁹ about current legislation from his work. He works _____ ¹⁰ in the city and he often meets members of the local council.

JANE   You need _____ ¹¹ who knows about sports.

FRANK   Well, Lester knows _____ ¹² about winter sports, he's a fanatic! I'm sure he's been skiing _____ ¹³ you can in Europe!

JANE   Is there _____ ¹⁴ who knows about sciences?

FRANK   Yes, Mary. And she also knows _____ ¹⁵ about theatre. She's got an amazing memory.

JANE   Great! Sounds like you've got _____ ¹⁶ covered. Good luck!

D   Advice from the Professor

A student wants to do a research degree and is talking to a university teacher in the coffee bar. Complete the dialogue by crossing out the wrong expression in each case.

STUDENT   Hello Professor Ramsey. Would you like *some / any* ⁰ coffee?

PROFESSOR   Yes, please.

STUDENT   Milk and sugar?

PROFESSOR   Just *a little / a few* ¹ milk, but *any / no* ² sugar. Oh, and a biscuit, please!

STUDENT   I'm afraid there aren't *any / some* ³. I've looked *everywhere / somewhere* ⁴ but I couldn't find any.

PROFESSOR   That's all right. I shouldn't really eat *anything / nothing* ⁵ between meals.

STUDENT   Please sit down *anywhere / nowhere* ⁶ that you'd like, Professor Ramsey. May I ask you *some / any* ⁷ questions about doing a research degree?

PROFESSOR   Sure. Do you know *much / many* ⁸ about what's involved?

STUDENT   Well, I've thought *a lot of / a lot* ⁹ about it. I've read *everything / something* ¹⁰ on the university website and I've also spoken to *a few / a little* ¹¹ students who have already started.

PROFESSOR   Have you read *much / many* ¹² research papers?

STUDENT   Well, we had to read *a lot of / a lot* ¹³ them for our degree project.

PROFESSOR   And have you written *any / some* ¹⁴ articles?

STUDENT   *A few / A little* ¹⁵, but *none / nothing* ¹⁶ that have been published, I'm afraid.

PROFESSOR   Hmm… Well, you're not an ideal candidate, but you can take the preparatory course, and I'll take a decision after that.

OVER TO YOU Now go to page 124.

20 Comparative and superlative forms
Adjectives: *tall, taller, tallest*

1 Here are some examples of sentences with **comparative** and **superlative adjectives**:

> The queue was *longer* than I expected.
> This is the *saddest* story I've ever heard.

2 **Short adjectives**
We make the **comparative and superlative form** of adjectives of one syllable by adding **-er** and **-est**:

tall	→	tall**er**	→	tall**est**
cheap	→	cheap**er**	→	cheap**est**

3 If the adjective ends in **-e**, we add **-r** and **-st**:

nice	→	nice**r**	→	nice**st**

4 If the adjective ends in one vowel and one consonant, we double the consonant and add **-er** and **-est**:

big	→	big**ger**	→	big**gest**
hot	→	hot**ter**	→	hot**test**

5 **Long adjectives**
If the adjective ends in **-y**, change the **y** to **i** and add **-er** and **-est**:

pretty	→	prett**ier**	→	prett**iest**
happy	→	happ**ier**	→	happ**iest**

6 A few forms are irregular:

good	→	**better**	→	**best**
bad	→	**worse**	→	**worst**
far	→	**further**	→	**furthest**

Also note the irregular comparative and superlative forms of the quantifiers **little**, **much** and **many**:

little	→	**less**	→	**least**
much	→	**more**	→	**most**
many	→	**more**	→	**most**

7 We normally make the comparative and superlative of other adjectives with **more** and **most**:

Adjectives ending in **-ing** e.g. **boring**, **interesting**
Adjectives ending in **-ed** e.g. **tired**, **settled**, **annoyed**
Adjectives ending in **-ful** e.g. **careful**, **helpful**
Adjectives ending in **-less** e.g. **useless**, **hopeless**
Long adjectives e.g. **practical**, **expensive**

> That was the *most boring* book I've ever read!
> This book is *more expensive* than that one.

> We can make a negative comparative with **no**:
> Their flat is **no bigger** than ours.
> The clothes in this shop are **no more expensive** than those in the market.

TIP

8 We use **adjectives** with nouns and pronouns. They describe the people or things we are talking about.

Grammar in action

1 We use a **comparative adjective + than** to compare one person or thing to say how they are different. We might talk about the appearance or character of people we know:

> Tim is taller than the other boys.
> Our new neighbours are more pleasant than the old ones.

2 We can use a **comparative adjective** with **than all the other / any / anything / ever** to compare one person or thing with every other thing in the same group:

> This TV is more expensive than all the others.
> This is a better price than any of the others.

3 We use **the** + a **superlative adjective** when we compare a person or thing with all of the group they are in. We want to say that one of the people or things is 'more … than the others'.

> This TV is the most expensive.
> This is the best price.

4 We can add more detail to the comparison using **much, far, a lot, a bit/little**. We might do this if we want to make it very clear which person we're talking about in a group sentence:

Tim is a bit taller than the other boys.

Sally is much taller than the other girls

5 We don't have to mention the second part of the comparison when we can understand it from the rest of the sentence:

> The other boys are tall but Tim is a bit taller.

A Different cars

Look at the table below and complete the sentences using comparative and superlative forms of *long, short, big, small, light, heavy* and *expensive,* and *than*.

	length (m)	engine size (cc)	weight (kg)	seats	price (£)
Wheeler	3.9	1198	1,014	5	8,000
Autostar	4.1	1390	1,182	4	12,000
Cruiser	4.2	1781	1,359	5	14,000

0 Length: The Autostar is _longer than_ the Wheeler but _shorter than_ the Cruiser.

0 Length: The Cruiser is _the longest_ of the three.

1 Engine size: The engine in the Autostar is .... the one in the Cruiser; the Wheeler has .... engine.

2 Weight: The Autostar is .... the Cruiser; in fact, the Cruiser is .... of the three.

3 Seats: The Wheeler and the Cruiser have a .... seating capacity .... the Autostar.

4 Price: The Autostar is .... the Wheeler, but the Cruiser is .... of the three.

B School report

Complete this school report about a sister and brother with the correct comparative or superlative form of the words in brackets. Use *than* where necessary.

Jenny and Bob are _happier than_ **0** (happy) they were at the beginning of the year because they are .... **1** (settled). They are .... **2** (good) most of their classmates at maths and science. In fact, in the last test Jenny got .... **3** (good) mark. They are a bit .... **4** (weak) in languages but certainly not .... **5** (weak) in the class.

C Comments about friends

Complete the comments using comparative or superlative forms of the adjectives given.

0 Amy is / bright / the rest of the class. Some people say she's / intelligent girl in the whole school.
    Amy is brighter than the rest of the class. Some people say she's the most
    intelligent girl in the whole school.

1 I find Clive / interesting / Tom. His jokes are some of / funny / ones I've ever heard.

....

2 Greta is / good / most people at chess but she isn't / good / player in the club.

....

3 Loïc is / lazy / person I've ever met. He does / little / anyone else.

....

9 We use **adverbs** with verbs, adjectives or other adverbs. They tell us how, when, where or how often something happens:

> Jane drives **slowly**.

(For more information on adverbs, see p. 86.)

10 We make the **comparative** and **superlative** form of some short **adverbs** with **-er** and **-est**:

fast	→	**faster**	→	**fastest**
hard	→	**harder**	→	**hardest**
early	→	**earlier**	→	**earliest**
soon	→	**sooner**	→	**soonest**

11 We make the **comparative** and **superlative** form of most **adverbs** with **more** and **most**:

clearly	→ **more clearly**	→ **most clearly**	
frequently	→ **more frequently**	→ **most frequently**	

12 Some common **adverbs** have irregular **comparative** and **superlative** forms:

well	→	**better**	→	**best**
badly	→	**worse**	→	**worst**
far	→	**further**	→	**furthest**
hard	→	**harder**	→	**hardest**
late	→	**later**	→	**latest**

13 We can use **less** or **least** with a **comparative adjective** or **adverb** to compare things in a negative way:

> Older people are **less mobile** than youngsters.
> He plays golf **less frequently** than he used to.
> James is **the least capable** of all the candidates.

TIP

When we use **better** to talk about someone who has been ill, it usually means 'well again', e.g.:

> My mum was ill last month but she's **better** now. (= she's all right now)

Grammar in action

⑥ We use **comparative adverbs** to compare actions, for example when we talk about the way people do things:

> When Phil had his accident, he was driving a lot faster than the speed limit. These days, he drives much more slowly and carefully. He says he used to arrive at work earlier but it's better to be safe than sorry.

D Comparing people in a group

Use the words given to express a similar meaning.

0 Tom is the fastest runner in the school.

Nobody else in the school / run / fast / Tom. *Nobody in the school runs faster than Tom.*

1 Everybody sings better than me.

I sing / badly / everybody else. ....

2 She used to visit us more often.

Nowadays, she visits us / often / she used to. ....

3 Nobody takes more care of their plants than my mother.

My mother looks after her plants / careful / than anyone else. ....

4 Rod was the first to arrive.

Rod arrived / early / everyone else. ....

E How are things different from 20 years ago?

Complete this dialogue with the correct comparative or superlative expression, using the words in brackets where they are given.

PAUL   Do you think life is ___easier than___ [0] (easy) it was 20 years ago?

WENDY   It depends. Nowadays, there's _____ [1] (much) work for some people and _____ [2] (little) for others compared with before. Typically, people in jobs like mine work _____ [3] (long) we did when I was young.

PAUL   But you're still young.

WENDY   Well, all right, but I'm _____ [4] (old) in the shop where I work. I worry _____ [5] (much) about the future and I feel like I work _____ [6] (hard) for the same wages. Everything is _____ [7] (expensive) and _____ [8] (complicated) when we were younger.

PAUL   That's a funny attitude when the standard of living in this country is _____ [9] (high) that it has ever been!

WENDY   Is it? It doesn't feel like that to me!

PAUL   You used to talk _____ [10] (optimistic) than that. My mother said that you were _____ [11] (positive) person she knew when we were young. Sorry, I mean when we were _____ [12] (young).

WENDY   But things have changed. Don't you think that things nowadays are _____ [13] (bad) than they were?

PAUL   I personally take things _____ [14] (easy) now than I did before . Now that I'm _____ [15] (old) and _____ [16] (wise) I'm _____ [17] (relaxed).

WENDY   I suppose if I could relax, I'd see things _____ [18] (positive). Maybe it's me that's changed.

PAUL   That's certainly a _____ [19] (good) way to look at things!

F How to do things better

Complete the captions with comparative adverbs.

0 He should run ___faster___ .

1 He should hit the ball _____ .

2 She should jump _____ .

3 She should arrive _____ .

OVER TO YOU Now go to page 124.

21 (Not) as … as, enough, too
They ran as fast as they could, but not fast enough.

1 We use **(not) as … as** to say that people or things are (not) the same in some way. We can use an adjective, adverb or quantifier with **(not) as … as** like this:

*Their flat is **as big as** ours.*
*They ran **as fast as** they could.*
*This time there **aren't as many** people **as** last time.*
*You should save **as much as** possible.*

2 We can also use **(not) the same + noun + as** to compare people or things in this way:

*Their flat is **the same size as** ours.*
*The chairs should be **the same height as** the table.*

3 We use **enough** before nouns:

*I'm afraid we haven't got **enough milk**.*

We use **enough** after adjectives and adverbs:

*This car isn't **comfortable enough** and the other one doesn't go **fast enough**.*

4 We can use **enough** without a noun when the meaning is clear:

*Let's stop work now. We've done **enough**.*
(= enough work)

5 A phrase with **enough** can continue with **for** and a noun or pronoun:

*Have we got **enough** bread **for breakfast**?*
*This coffee isn't strong **enough for me**.*

6 A phrase with **enough** can continue with an infinitive:

*I haven't got **enough space to pack** my hairdryer.*
*This bike is **light enough to carry** as hand baggage.*

We can also combine phrases with **for** and **to**:

*There wasn't **enough** time **for me to finish** my dinner.*

Grammar in action

1 We use **as … as** to compare two things when we are making a choice. This might be when we are deciding what to buy:

I don't think I want a vase as tall as that red one, but the small vase is as expensive as the tall ones. I'm not sure I want to pay as much as that.

2 Many common idioms in English use **as … as** to emphasize an adjective in a description. Here are some examples:

He was as pleased as Punch. (= very pleased)
Jo's face went as red as a lobster. (= very red)
Coffee should be as dark as night, as strong as death, and as sweet as love.

3 We use **enough** in positive sentences to say that we have the right amount of something:

We've got enough apples to last until January.

> Informally, we can use the phrase **I've had enough of + noun** to express frustration or impatience.
> *I've had enough of this awful weather!*

TIP

4 We often use **enough** in a negative sentence to say that we do not have as much of something as we need:

We don't have enough money to pay the bills.

5 We use **enough** in questions to check that someone else has what they need. For example, we can make sure a guest is comfortable:

*Have you got **enough** room? ~ Yes, I'm OK.*
*Have you had **enough** potatoes? ~ Plenty, thanks.*

A   A new language course.

Complete the conversation using the prompts and *as … as* **or** *the same … as*.

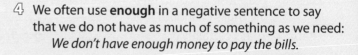

GEOFF   So how's your course, Tom?
TOM   It's OK. Our new teacher ‿‿is as good as the old one.‿‿⁰ (be good / the old one).
GEOFF   Are you learning a lot?
TOM   Yes, but not ....¹ (much / before).
GEOFF   How good is your Russian now?
TOM   Well, I can ....² (understand / well / the other students) but I can't ....³ (speak / fluently / them).
GEOFF   Are you progressing ....⁴ (quickly / you hoped)?

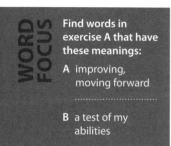

TOM   Not really. Though I've had a lot of work recently so I haven't been attending

.... [5] (many / lessons / I wanted).

We've got .... [6] (amount of homework / last year)
though, so I hope I'll keep improving if I work at home, too.

GEOFF Are you using .... [7] (books / before)?

TOM   No, this course is the next level, so it's not .... [8]
(easy / the one last year). But that's OK because I like a challenge!

B   Always complaining!

Lewis never seems to have the right amount of the things he needs.
Complete these sentences with *enough* and one of the words from the box.

| often   well   air   fast   flour   large   money   sweet   strong |

0 This hot chocolate isn't ~~sweet enough~~ to drink.

1 Have we got .... to make a cake?

2 The bookshelf isn't .... to hold all those books.

3 Do you think there's .... in my bicycle tyres?

4 Have we got .... for a new TV?

5 Our internet connection isn't .... to download a film.

6 We haven't got a vase that's .... for all those flowers.

7 His room is a mess. He doesn't tidy it ....

8 The old hoover didn't clean the carpet ....

C   Things I said today

Complete the sentences with *enough* and the word in brackets, making any other
necessary changes.

0 These shoes are size 9 but Peter takes size 10.

The shoes are not ~~big enough for~~ (big) Peter.

1 It takes half an hour to walk to the station. The train leaves in 45 minutes.

We have .... (time) walk to the station and catch the train.

2 People usually eat two sausages and we have 10.

We have .... (sausages) five people.

3 It isn't very light so we can't take any photos.

It isn't .... (light) take any photos.

4 The bed is 180 cm but Sally is 185 cm tall.

The bed isn't .... (long) Sally.

5 We can't go to the beach because it's a bit cold.

It isn't .... (warm) go to the beach.

6 He doesn't play his music loudly. It doesn't annoy the neighbours.

He doesn't play his music .... (loudly) to annoy the neighbours.

7 **Too slow** and **not quick enough** mean the same thing. We can use **too** with an adjective, an adverb or quantifier like this:

> too big   too quickly
> too much noise   too few people

8 We use **too** before an adjective or adverb:

> My new shoes are **too small**. I bought them **too quickly**.

We use **too much**, **too many**, **too few** and **too little**. before a noun. In these sentences, we can leave out the noun if the meaning is clear:

> We bought **too much paint**.
> We thought we hadn't bought enough paint, but we'd bought **too much**. (too much = too much paint)

9 A phrase with **too** can continue with **for** and a noun or pronoun:

> This weather is **too hot for my dad**.
> There are **too few chairs for all these people**.
> The teacher spoke **too fast for me**.

10 A phrase with **too** can continue with an infinitive:

> It's **too hot to sit** in the sun.
> There are **too few players to make** a team.

When the subject of the sentence is (in meaning) the object of the infinitive, we omit the object, so:

> The soup was **too hot to eat**.
> (NOT ~~The soup was too hot to eat it.~~)

> In negative statements, people sometimes use **too** with a meaning similar to **very**:
> I don't know **too much** about computers.
> (= I don't know very much ...)
> She didn't look **too happy**. (= ... look very happy)

Grammar in action

⑥ We use **too** to mean 'more than enough' or when we have more of something than we need. When we go shopping, we can talk about whether the things we look at are suitable:

> I want a simple camera. This one has too many buttons.
> That jacket is too big for you.
> I don't want anything too expensive. I can't pay more than about £40.

D   **Vehicle problems**

Complete the sentences with *too* so that they correspond to the information given.

0   The speed limit is 100kph but Gregg's driving at 35kph.
Gregg's driving ...... *too slowly* ....

1   The car holds five people but there were seven in it.
There were .... people in the car.

2   Max isn't old enough to have a motorbike.
Max is .... to have a motorbike.

3   John's car was parked for two hours but he had only paid for 45 minutes.
John's car was parked for ....

4   We haven't got enough petrol for a drive to the coast.
We've got .... petrol for a drive to the coast.

5   The tyres need more air.
There's .... air in the tyres.

6   There aren't enough service stations on this road.
There are .... service stations on this road.

7   Jenny did very badly in the exam.
Jenny didn't do .... in the exam.

E   The imperfect holiday

Complete the conversation using the words in brackets and *as … as*, *enough* or *too*, and adding *to* or *for* where necessary.

SUE   Did you enjoy your holiday?

PIPPA   It didn't go _____*as well as*_____ ⁰ we'd hoped.

LUCY   Things started badly at the airport. There weren't _____ ¹ (people) checking the luggage so the queue was enormous.

SUE   But was the flight OK?

PIPPA   It was one of those planes with the seats _____ ² (close together) possible so you can't stretch your legs. However, the flight was _____ ³ (short) so it wasn't a big problem.

LUCY   And there were far _____ ⁴ (many) young men who had packed far _____ ⁵ (much) in their hand luggage, so their bags were _____ ⁶ (big) to go in the lockers.

SUE   What about the hotel?

PIPPA   It was all right, I suppose, but we couldn't change the air conditioning, so it was _____ ⁷ (cold) me.

LUCY   And the food wasn't _____ ⁸ (wonderful) the website claimed. It was much _____ ⁹ (oily). In any case, every meal was rushed so there was never _____ ¹⁰ (time) really enjoy it.

SUE   Did you visit the old town?

PIPPA   Yes, it was all organized in groups, but the groups were _____ ¹¹ (big). And our guide didn't speak _____ ¹² (loudly), so it was impossible to hear her.

LUCY   The cathedral was wonderful, though. It really is _____ ¹³ (spectacular) everybody says.

SUE   And the night life?

PIPPA   Great, although the bars are always _____ ¹⁴ (noisy) a serious conversation.

LUCY   Nobody wants a serious conversation on holiday. We obviously enjoyed it because we were out so late that most days we got up _____ ¹⁵ (late) have breakfast.

PIPPA   On the last day, we went shopping and we bought you this T-shirt. I hope it's _____ ¹⁶ (big) you.

SUE   Oh, how nice! Yes, it's my size.

OVER TO YOU Now go to page 124.

1 We use **adverbs** with verbs, adjectives or other adverbs. They tell us how, when, where or how often something happens:

*He speaks **quickly**.*
*Dan played football **yesterday**.*
*Has Jo gone **outside**?*
*I **always** eat breakfast.*

2 **Adverbs of frequency**
Adverbs of frequency tell us how often something happens. They include **always**, **ever**, **often**, **usually**, **sometimes**, **seldom/rarely**, **never**.

*Jim is **always** the first to arrive.*
*Have you **ever** played squash?*

Adverbs of frequency usually come after **be** and auxiliaries, but before the main verb.

Sometimes and **usually** can also go at the beginning of the sentence:

***Sometimes** we play cricket on Friday.*
***Usually** Laura and I walk to school together.*

We can also use **every day**, **once** or phrases like **twice/three times a week** to talk about frequency. These can go at the beginning or end of the sentence:

***Every Thursday** we have lunch together.*
*I play bridge **twice a week**.*

3 **Adverbs of time**
Adverbs of time explain when something happens. They include **today**, **yesterday**, **tomorrow**, **early**, **late**. These adverbs usually go at the end of the sentence:

*What are you doing **today**?*
*We are leaving **tomorrow**.*

Today, **yesterday**, **tomorrow** and **afterwards** can also go at the beginning of the sentence:

***Yesterday** it rained all day.*
***Today** we studied the life of frogs.*

Common phrases that are used as adverbs of time are:

> on Friday, etc.   last Friday, etc.
> next Friday, etc.   in January, etc.
> in 1999, etc.   for two years, etc.

4 **Adverbs of place**
Adverbs of place tell us where something is. They include **here**, **there**, **in**, **out**, **away**, **abroad**, **back**, **around**, **somewhere**, **everywhere**, **outside**, **inside**, **upstairs**, **downstairs**. They usually go at the end of the sentence:

*We're going to meet **here/there**.*

*Her grandparents live **abroad**.*

We can use many phrases as adverbs of place:

> on the roof   in the park   at the bus stop
> along the road   to Paris   into the room

5 **Adverbs of manner**
Adverbs of manner tell us how something is done. They usually go after the verb, or after an object:

*She sings **beautifully**.*
*His sister doesn't speak French **well**.*

Short adverbs ending in **-ly** can also go between the subject and the verb if they are not the main information:

*I **quickly** realized that there was a problem.*
*The examiner **quietly** helped Marie to gather her papers.*

6 When there is more than one adverb after the verb, the normal order is manner, place, time:

*Everyone went **slowly upstairs**. (manner, place)*
*We worked **hard in the garden yesterday**. (manner, place, time)*

Grammar in action

1 We can use **adverbs of frequency** to talk about our habits, and how often we do things in the present, or have done them in the past:

When I was at school I always studied before exams but I hardly ever got good marks. I rarely failed though.

2 We use **adverbs of manner** to describe a process, or explain how to make something. For example, when we are cooking:

It's a good idea to read the recipe carefully. If it's the first time, you should follow the recipe exactly and mix the ingredients thoroughly.

3 We can use **adverbs of time** to tell someone about the progress of a job over a number of days:

On Saturday we worked outside and painted the doors and windows there. We worked inside today.

4 We use **adverbs of place** when we want to describe where something or somebody is:

My father isn't here at the moment, he's away. I think he's abroad.

A Describing people's habits

Put the words in the correct order to make sentences.

0 always / arrived / early / has
Jenny _has always arrived early_ .

1 upstairs / sleeps / never
Grandfather _____ .

2 abroad / holidays / take / rarely / their
They _____ .

3 bed / ever / go / late / to / you
Do _____ ?

4 badly / dogs / often / the / treats
He _____ .

5 hard / Larry / try / usually
Does _____ ?

6 every / goes / Scotland / to / week
Adam _____ .

B A quiet village life

Complete this radio interview by putting the expressions in brackets in the correct order.

JASON Today we have a special guest in the studio, someone who _has worked_ _successfully in education and in publishing_ 0 (has / worked / in education and in publishing / successfully), Karen Lanchester. Thank you for _____ 1 (coming / this morning / to the studio).

KAREN My pleasure, Jason.

JASON You _____ 2 (been / in the news / often / have) recently. We seem to see your photo _____ 3 (every day / in the papers). And we saw you on television last Saturday.

KAREN That's because my latest novel _____ 4 (come out / has / just).

JASON Do you ever find that you have more work than time?

KAREN Well, I find that interruptions are the main problem, so I spent last year living _____ 5 (quietly / in a little village).

JASON Were you there for the whole year?

KAREN More or less. I _____ 6 (at weekends / occasionally / went / to London).

JASON Did you stay in the village all the time?

KAREN Yes, but I didn't stay in the house from morning to night. I _____ 7 (for a walk / sometimes / went) in the woods.

JASON And did you look after yourself?

KAREN No, a young woman _____ 8 (to the house / came / twice a week) and kept the place tidy, but she knew that I needed peace and quiet, so she _____ 9 (ever / hardly / spoke) to me.

JASON Fine. Now I think it's time for you to tell us a little about your novel.

KAREN Well, it's about a woman who lives _____ 10 (for a whole year / happily / in a village).

7 Adverbs of probability

Adverbs of probability, e.g. **certainly**, **probably**, **definitely**, can go between the subject and the verb after a positive auxiliary and before a negative auxiliary:

> You **certainly** made your position very clear.
> They'll **probably** change their minds.
> They **definitely** won't arrive on time.

However, **maybe** and **perhaps** usually go at the beginning of the sentence, e.g.:

> Perhaps/Maybe they'll like each other.

8 Adverbs of degree

We can use adverbs of degree to change the strength of other adverbs and adjectives. They go before the adjective. Here are some adverbs of degree which make adverbs and adjectives stronger:

> very   really   extremely   incredibly   absolutely

> I'm **really** excited about the new James Bond film. (stronger than I'm excited about …)

Here are some adverbs of degree which make adverbs and adjectives weaker:

> slightly   a bit   quite   fairly   rather

> He was **a bit** upset that he wasn't invited to the party. (not as strong as He was upset …)

9 Adverbs of completeness

We can use some adverbs to describe how complete an action is. These include **completely**, **totally**, **perfectly**, **virtually**, **practically**, **almost**, **hardly**, **scarcely**. They go between the subject and the verb, or after an auxiliary:

> I **completely** forgot her birthday. (= I didn't think of it at all.)
> We have **virtually** finished the project. (= We have finished most of it.)
> You'll **hardly** have time for any lunch. (= You'll have almost no time.)

Grammar in action

⑤ We can use **adverbs of probability** to talk about how certain, or uncertain, our plans and arrangements are:
> When we're in New York, we'll probably visit the Guggenheim Museum. Perhaps we'll take one of those boat trips on the Hudson.

⑥ We can use **adverbs of degree** to compare two or more people or things:
> John dances quite well, but Joanna dances really well.
> Children learn incredibly fast, whereas adults learn fairly slowly.

⑦ We can use **adverbs of degree** and **completeness** to comment on the way someone or something works:
> My watch is old, but it works perfectly well.
> Brian is extremely conscientious and is practically never ill or late.

C   Peter and Simon lead very different lives

Peter likes the quiet life, while Simon likes excitement. Underline the more likely adverb of degree in each case.

0   Peter didn't want to go to work today because he was feeling _rather_/extremely ill.

0   Simon had to go to hospital today because he was rather/_extremely_ ill.

1   Peter had a cup of coffee because he was _really/a bit_ tired.

2   Simon fell asleep at his desk because he was _really/a bit_ tired.

3   Peter was _very/fairly_ happy because he found a £5 note yesterday.

4   Simon was _very/fairly_ happy because he won a car yesterday.

5   Peter likes to drive _quite/Incredibly_ fast but never breaks the speed limit.

6   Simon is a very dangerous driver because he likes to drive _quite/incredibly_ fast.

D Talking about certainty and uncertainty

Read this email from Matt to his sister Jas about his plans for the summer. Circle the correct word.

> Hi Jas,
>
> How are things? Just to let you know my plans for the summer.
>
> Well, I think I'll *maybe /(probably)/ perhaps*⁰ come home next week. I'm not sure exactly when yet, but *definitely / probably / maybe*¹ it'll be next Monday. Tim is coming with me for a couple of days. Then we're *perhaps / maybe / definitely*² going to Spain for a week or two to relax. His parents have a flat there, so we'll *maybe / probably / perhaps*³ stay with them because it'll be free! When we come back I'll *perhaps / definitely / maybe*⁴ need to get a job to earn some money! *Probably / Certainly / Perhaps*⁵ I'll go back to the café I worked in last year– *maybe / definitely / certainly*⁶ they'll have some work for me again. Let's hope so!
>
> What about you? Have you *probably / definitely / maybe*⁷ decided to get married? You *maybe / certainly / perhaps*⁸ didn't take long to make up your mind. I'll *definitely / perhaps / maybe*⁹ come to the wedding and *certainly / probably / maybe*¹⁰ I'll even wear a suit! You know how much I hate them though!
>
> Take care. See you soon. Love, Matt

E A foreign trip

Ryan and Lyn are discussing holidays. Complete their conversation by filling each gap with two of the three expressions in brackets.

Inland means 'away from the sea'. **WORD FOCUS**

RYAN   Do you ___always go___⁰ (always, go, perhaps) abroad for your holidays?

LYNN   No, we stay _____¹ (at home, ever, most years). Foreign holidays _____² (are, never, usually) exhausting and we _____³ (definitely, fairly, prefer) a quiet life. How about you?

RYAN   We haven't _____⁴ (been, never, often) abroad but we went _____⁵ (seldom, last year, to Spain).

LYNN   Isn't it full of tourists?

RYAN   No, Spain is a _____⁶ (big, perfectly, very) country and the tourists tend to be _____⁷ (always, in the summer, on the coast). We stayed mostly inland so we managed to avoid the tourist parts. We went through some villages that were _____⁸ (empty, practically, probably) because a lot of people have moved to the towns, but the people who were living there were _____⁹ (absolutely, delighted, delightful) to see visitors. They _____¹¹ (made, certainly, maybe) made us very welcome.

LYNN   Do you speak Spanish?

RYAN   My wife speaks it _____¹¹ (fluent, fluently, quite), and she also speaks some Catalan. That was helpful when we were in Barcelona, in Catalunya, because it is _____¹² (different, differently, rather) from the rest of Spain.

LYNN   Isn't that where that famous cathedral is?

RYAN   Yes, it's called the Sagrada Família. It's _____¹³ (absolutely, enormously, enormous) though not _____¹⁴ (attractive, particular, particularly), if you ask me.

LYNN   Would you like to go back to Spain?

RYAN   Yes, we _____¹⁵ (certainly, hardly, want) to go back, but it _____¹⁶ (maybe, probably, will) be a few years before we can afford to go abroad again.

OVER TO YOU Now go to page 124.

1 We use **so** + **auxiliary verb** + **subject** in a positive sentence to say that something is true of two subjects:

> *I'm excited about the wedding! ~ **So am I**.*
> *Jenny's invited Martin to the party. ~ **So has Mark**.*

If there is no auxiliary verb, we use **do/does/did**:

> *Oliver lives in Leeds. ~ **So does Alex**.*

2 Instead of **so am I**, we can say **I am, too**.

> *Oliver lives in Leeds. ~ **Alex does, too**.*

3 We use **neither** + **auxiliary verb** + **subject** in a negative sentence:

> *Joe can't speak German. ~ **Neither can Megan**.*
> *Hans doesn't understand Chinese. ~ **Neither do I**.*

> Notice that if the main verb is positive, we use a negative auxiliary, and if the main verb is negative, we use a positive auxiliary.

4 Instead of **neither am I**, we can say **I'm not, either**:

> *Hans doesn't understand Chinese. ~ **I don't, either**.*

(For information on **either … or** and **neither … nor**, see p. 102.)

Grammar in action

1 We can use **so** and **too** when we want to add another fact or more information to a conversation without repeating the whole sentence. We can use them to talk about relatives, friends, and colleagues:

> *Greg likes Jack and his brother does, too. ~ Yes, I play football with Jack and so does Greg's brother.*
> *Liz is very helpful and so is her sister. ~ Yes, they both helped us with the last party and Philip did, too.*

2 We can use **neither** and **either** when we want to add another negative fact or idea to a conversation. We can use them to talk about things we don't do or don't like:

> *I don't each much meat and neither does my husband. My parents don't like blue cheese, and I don't, either.*

3 We can use **so**, **too**, **neither** and **either** in short answers when we want to agree with what someone is saying or say that our experience is the same:

> *I don't like pizza. ~ Neither do I.*
> *We loved that book. ~ So did we.*

4 We can use **so**, **too**, **neither** and **either** with a possessive subject (**mine**, **Ben's**, **ours**, etc.) to compare the things we own with someone else's:

> *Emma's birthday is in April. ~ So is mine!*
> *Her party was brilliant last year. ~ Ian's was, too.*

A   Talking about your family

Read this email from John telling his friend about his family. Choose the correct answer.

Dear Talla,

You asked about my family, so here's a bit more information. I go to a secondary school in Manchester, and ......*so*......⁰ (so/either/too) do my two brothers, Jake and Nathan. I love my school, and they do, ...¹ (so/too/either). I don't like art , and Jake doesn't, ...² (neither/too/either). I prefer science and ....³ (too/neither/so) does Nathan. You said you enjoyed swimming and I do, ...⁴ (neither/so/too). And you also said you didn't like football. I don't, ...⁵ (too/neither/either), and ....⁶ (neither/either/so) do my brothers. We all hate it! My father loves it and ....⁷ (too/either/so) does my mother, but they only watch it on TV, they don't play!

I'm going on holiday next week and I think you said that you are, ...⁸ (so/too/either). Write to me when you get back.

Your friend, John

B Do I know you?

Two students have just met at university. Complete the gaps using *so* or *neither* and the correct auxiliary.

SARAH   Hi, I'm Sarah. Where are you from?

HELEN   I was born in Wales.

SARAH   That's funny, _____so was I!_____ 0

HELEN   But I didn't like my town.

SARAH   .... 1.

HELEN   When's your birthday Sarah?

SARAH   In January.

HELEN   .... 2.

SARAH   But I don't really like birthday parties.

HELEN   .... 3. I prefer to go to the cinema with a few friends.

SARAH   .... 4. Though I don't know many people here yet.

HELEN   .... 5. I want to join the basketball team.

SARAH   .... 6. Did you play at school?

HELEN   Yes, I played for my school and the Welsh team.

SARAH   .... 7. Did you play in the final last summer?

HELEN   Yes, I did.

SARAH   .... 8. I think we met then.

HELEN   Yes, ... 9.

C Staff room gossip

Two teachers are talking about their pupils. Complete the sentences using the words in brackets and the correct auxiliary.

MR REID   My class this year is better than last year.

MS PIKE   _____So is mine_____ 0 (mine, so), though the students aren't as quiet as I'd like.

MR REID   .... 1 (mine, neither). How many have you got? I've got 31.

MS PIKE   .... 2 (I, too). I think that your class has one or two brothers and sisters of some of my pupils.

MR REID   .... 3 (I, so). For example, I have Billy Jarvis, who's very good at maths.

MS PIKE   .... 4 (his sister, so), Holly, who's in my class. Then there's Isabel Pinter, who writes wonderful essays.

MR REID   .... 5 (her brother, too). But he can't draw at all.

MS PIKE   .... 6 (Isabel, either). A lot of these things run in families. Last year, I had a boy who drew very good faces and .... 7 (his older sister, so). She was in my class the year before.

MR REID   Have you got anybody called Smithson? I've got Philip Smithson and he doesn't take an interest in anything.

MS PIKE   .... 8 (his brother, neither). Well, they can't all be brilliant.

MR REID   No, but they could all show a bit of interest.

Connecting adverbs
First, next, then, etc.; actually, fortunately, etc.; only, even

5 We use **first, second**, etc., **then, next, later, afterwards, meanwhile, finally** to show the order that something happens in. These adverbs tend to go at the beginning of the sentence:

*Mum, can we go and play football? ~ Not now. **First** you must tidy your room. **Then** you have to do your homework. **Afterwards** you can go and play football.*

6 We use **actually, apparently, (un)fortunately, frankly, hopefully, luckily, obviously** to say what we think about an action or situation. These adverbs tend to go at the beginning of the sentence:

***Luckily**, the train wasn't very crowded.*
(= It's lucky that the train …)
***Obviously**, someone's not telling the truth.*
(= It's obvious.)
*Some people think that Fred's Canadian, but **actually**, he's never been to Canada.* (= … in fact …)

7 We use **only** to point to one part of a sentence. It normally goes before the information that it refers to (the subject), and explains the limit of a number or amount:

***Only** one person paid £100.*
(= not more than one person…)
*One person paid **only** £100.*
(= not more than £100)

When **only** points to another part of the sentence (not the subject), it goes between the subject and the verb or after an auxiliary:

*One person **only** paid £100.*
(= didn't pay more than £100)

8 We use **even** to say that information is surprising or unusual. It can go in the same positions as **only**:

***Even** my grandmother stayed up to watch the match.*
(= It was surprising that my grandmother also …)
*Raj reads everything. He **even** reads cornflake packets.* (= It is unusual for anybody to read …)

Grammar in action

⑤ We can use adverbs like **then, next**, etc. to give instructions, or tell someone how to do something, for example, how to make an omelette:

First, break a couple of eggs into a bowl. Next, add a pinch of salt and then beat the eggs with a fork. Meanwhile, you should heat a frying pan with a little oil. Finally, turn the omelette onto a plate and enjoy!

⑥ We use adverbs like **then, next**, etc. when we want to tell a story or explain the order of events in the past, for example when we are telling someone what happened in a film or book:

I really enjoyed this book. First the children went to stay with their grandparents in an old house. Then they found a secret garden behind the house. Next they met a young boy who lived next door. Later they went to the garden with the boy and afterwards they …

⑦ We can use adverbs like **luckily, fortunately**, etc. to make judgements and give our opinions, express our feelings, and explain our thoughts on something:

Fortunately, Jack's operation was not too serious. Obviously he's pleased about the way things have gone. Apparently he should be back home in a few days.

D   Pointing to one thing

William is telling his mum about the friends he has made at his new job. Complete the sentences using *only* or *even*.

0   Henry goes to college on Mondays. He doesn't go on other days.

Henry ....*only*............ goes to college on Mondays.

1   Kerry eats vegetables, but she won't eat meat or fish.

Kerry .... eats vegetables.

2   John won £1.50 on the lottery last week! He didn't win any more than that.

John .... won £1.50.

3   I can't believe that Abigail can't drive! It's so easy!

Abigail can't .... drive!

4 Everyone was at the office party to welcome me. I was surprised to see the manager there, too!

.... the manager was at the office party.

E   Giving our opinion

Circle the correct adverb for each situation.

0 I needed to speak to Mr Thomas. *Frankly / Fortunately /* (*Unfortunately*) he wasn't in the office.

1 Jim tells people he's an engineer but *actually / hopefully / unfortunately* he's only a technician.

2 *Apparently / Frankly / Luckily* there's been an accident but nobody knows any details.

3 We don't know when the electrician's coming but *hopefully / actually / obviously* it will be one day this week.

4 The children haven't had anything to drink all morning so *actually / obviously / luckily* they're thirsty.

5 The fire was pretty serious but *hopefully / luckily / unfortunately* nobody was hurt, thank goodness.

WORD FOCUS

Actually means 'in fact.' We use it to emphasize a fact or what is true.

Apparently means 'according to what I have read or heard.'

Hopefully means 'what I hope will happen.'

Fortunately means 'by good luck.'

F   Going shopping

Eve and Jack are going shopping. Complete their conversation using one of the words from the box in each space.

> either   even   finally   first   hopefully   hopefully   meanwhile
> neither   obviously   ~~only~~   then   too   unfortunately

EVE   Jack, do you want to go shopping with me?

JACK   Let me finish what I'm doing. I ....*only*........ ⁰ need a few minutes. The thing is that I've never ordered anything online before.

EVE   .... ¹ have I.

JACK   .... ² it should be easy. They tell me that .... ³ children can manage these things.

EVE   Well, I can't help you so keep trying. .... ⁴, I'll make a shopping list.

(Later)

JACK   After lots of work I .... ⁵ sent the order! Have you made the shopping list?

EVE   Yes, ... ⁶ we need to go to the butcher's to buy some steak. .... ⁷ they've got some of that Scotch steak that was so good. I really enjoyed it last time.

JACK   I did, ... ⁸. Where do we need to go .... ⁹?

EVE   To the supermarket, because we need milk and water as well as fruit and vegetables.

JACK   If there are so many heavy things, ... ¹⁰ we need to go by car.

EVE   We could go in mine but .... ¹¹, it hasn't got much petrol in it.

JACK   Mine hasn't, ... ¹².

EVE   OK. We'll have to start by going to the petrol station.

OVER TO YOU Now go to page 125.

24 Prepositions (1)
Preposition + noun/adjective: *for sale, in love*, etc.

1 There are many useful phrases formed with **preposition + noun** or **preposition + adjective**. Here are some examples:

prep.	noun/adj.	prep.	noun/adj.
at	present	in	love
by	car	on	time
for	sale	out of	date

Are you going to Scotland by car?
My passport is out of date.

2 Some **preposition + noun** phrases include an article:

prep.	article	noun
at	the	front
in	a	hurry
in	the	end

Let's sit at the front so we can see the band.
We're in a hurry; we've got to catch a train.

Grammar in action

1 We use prepositional phrases to talk about where people and things are: **at home/school/work, on holiday, at the back end/front/bottom/top, in bed, in the way** (= blocking the way), **on the way** (= during the journey), **out of doors, in town, into town.**

> *Jack isn't at work. He's still in bed.*
> *I can't leave because your bags are in the way.*

2 We use the preposition **to** with some nouns to describe movement: **to school/work/bed/town, to the back/front/bottom/top.**

> *They have gone to school so I'm going to town this morning.*

> Note that **home** has no preposition for movement:
> *We went/came/arrived home early.*
> (NOT *to home*)
> TIP

3 When we give somebody directions, we often use prepositions with a noun to explain where a place is or how to get there:

> on the corner   next to the bank/post office etc.
> over the bridge   up/down/along the street
> through the gate

> *The post office is on the corner of George Street and the butcher's is next to the bank.*

4 We use the preposition **by** with a vehicle to talk about a means of transport:

> by bike   by bus   by car   by ferry
> by plane   by ship   by taxi   by tram
> by train   by underground

> *Is it cheaper to go by train or by bus?*
> *I never go into town by car.*

> If we use a possessive adjective to talk about the owner of the vehicle, we cannot use **by**; instead we use **on** with **bike** and **in** with **car**:
> *I never go into town in my car.* (NOT *by my car*)
> *Sara goes everywhere on her bike.* (NOT *by her bike*)
> TIP

5 We use certain prepositional phrases to tell stories, or when we are explaining a sequence of events:

> at first   at/in the beginning
> in the end   at last

> *At first Harry is an assistant in a music shop but in the end he becomes a famous musician.*

6 We use these prepositional phrases when we talk about shops and shopping:

> in/out of fashion   in/out of stock   in cash
> out of date   on sale   on offer
> by credit card   for sale

> *Hats are out of fashion.* (= Hats are not popular now.)
> *We have every size in stock.* (= Every size is available.)
> *Would you like to pay in cash or by credit card?*

7 When we are describing people, we use **with** to describe their features and **in** to describe their clothes:
> *He's the boy with long legs dressed in black.*
> *Who's that woman with red hair in the blue shirt?*

A Conversations overheard in a queue

Complete these mini-dialogues with a preposition.

0 Is Jane ___*at*___ work? ~ No, she's ___*on*___ holiday.

1 Do you like to be _____ doors? ~ Yes, I like to sit _____ the bottom of the garden.

2 Did you get _____ work on time? ~ Yes, I met Kate _____ the way to the station and she took me _____ her car.

3 Do you always go _____ school _____ bus? ~ No, sometimes I go _____ my bike.

4 Is that Jenny _____ the red jacket? ~ No, she's the one _____ the red hair.

5 Did they fall _____ love _____ the end? ~ Yes, but _____ first they hated each other!

6 Can I pay for this _____ credit card? ~ I'm afraid you can only pay _____ cash.

B Giving directions and talking about transport

Complete the dialogue using the prepositions in the box.

> at   by   by   down   on   next to   over

CHRIS   Excuse me, is there a coffee bar near here?

AVA   Yes, it's ___*next to*___ ⁰ the newsagent's. I'll tell you how to get there.

CHRIS   That would be great. Is it very far? Do I need to go _____ ¹ bus?

AVA   No, you could walk. Or you could go _____ ² tram, as it stops right outside.

CHRIS   I think I'll walk. Do I carry on _____ ³ this street?

AVA   Yes, and when you see the sports shop _____ ⁴ the corner, turn left. _____ ⁵ the end of that street, you need to go _____ ⁶ the bridge. Then you'll see the coffee bar in front of you!

C Talking about shops and fashion

Complete the dialogue by filling each gap with an expression from the box and the correct preposition.

> cash   credit card   the end   home   offer   stock   town

CLAIRE   I went ___*to town*___ ⁰ yesterday to do some shopping.

ISABEL   Did you see any nice skirts in the shops?

CLAIRE   Yes, there were some _____ ¹ at that big shop in the new mall.

ISABEL   Didn't you buy one, then?

CLAIRE   I wanted a black one, but my size was _____ ².

ISABEL   Did you buy anything?

CLAIRE   _____ ³ I bought a bag. But I nearly didn't buy it.

ISABEL   Why, what happened?

CLAIRE   I was going to pay _____ ⁴ but it turned out that I'd left my card _____ ⁵.

ISABEL   So how did you pay?

CLAIRE   I went to the bank to get the money and paid them _____ ⁶.

ISABEL   You're lucky to have money left so late in the month. I won't have any until we get paid next week.

3 After the verb **be**, an adjective can be followed by a **preposition** + **a noun phrase** (noun or pronoun):

adjective	preposition	noun (phrase)
afraid	of	dogs
sorry	for	the mess
pleased	with	her results

*My brother is **afraid of** spiders.*
*Are you **sorry for** your mistake?*
*She was **pleased with** the present.*

After the verb **be**, an adjective can also be followed by a **clause** or **to** + **verb**. In these cases, there is no preposition:

*Are you **sorry** (that) **you made a mistake**?*
*She was **pleased that we came early**.*
*She **was pleased to see** her cousins.*
*I was **afraid to tell** them the truth.*

> If a verb follows a preposition, we always use the *-ing* form, e.g.:
> *I'm tired **of telling** them to be careful.*
> *Who is responsible **for checking** the identity cards?*

4 Some nouns can be followed by a **preposition** + **noun phrase**:

noun	preposition	noun (phrase)
reason	for	the party
belief	in	ghosts
effect	on	my situation

*The festival was the **reason for** the traffic.*
*I don't take their **belief in** magic seriously.*
*Cars have a serious **effect on** the climate.*

Grammar in action

Ⓑ There are many **adjective + preposition** combinations that we can use to talk about feelings:

> angry/cross with   disappointed with
> annoyed with   pleased with   excited about
> curious about   happy about   sorry about
> worried about   tired of   afraid of
> fond of   sick of   proud of   jealous of
> sorry for   surprised at/by
> astonished at/by   interested in

Are you afraid of snakes? ~ Yes, I'm a bit worried about our holiday to Australia! ~ Oh don't worry. If you see one, I think you'll be more curious about them than scared. I was disappointed with my results. They were surprised at my refusal.

Ⓨ We can use an **adjective + preposition** to talk about someone's attitude (the way that they speak or feel):

> right/wrong about   honest about   polite to
> ready for   gentle with   responsible for
> rude to

I think I'm ready for the test. ~ Remember to be polite to the examiner.

⑩ We can also use an **adjective + preposition** to talk about similarity:

> identical to   the same as   similar to
> different from

Your eyes are the same as your mother's, but your hair is very different from hers.

⑪ We can use a **noun + preposition** to talk about someone's opinions, beliefs or feelings towards someone or something:

> attitude to/towards   reaction to   hope of
> opinion of/about   respect for   advice on
> belief in

I don't have a very good opinion of David. He has a very bad attitude to work and has very little respect for his colleagues.

⑫ We also use a **noun + preposition** to talk about the connection or relation between two things:

> reason for   effect on   trouble with
> difficulty in/with   result of   cause of
> rise/increase in   fall/reduction in

An increase in the price is the cause of the fall in sales.

D I'm worried about George

Complete the conversation using the correct prepositions.

WORD FOCUS

Find a phrase in exercise D that has this meaning:

I'm not surprised that …

....

JACK   I'm worried _about_ ⁰ George. He's usually so polite .... ¹ everyone, but yesterday he was so rude .... ² me when I saw him! It's just not like him.

LISA   That sounds very different .... ³ the George that I know. Can you think of a reason .... ⁴ him to be like this?

JACK   No, I was going to ask if you knew why his attitude .... ⁵ me had changed. Do you think I should talk to him? What's your advice .... ⁶ what I should do next?

LISA   Maybe it's his new job. I think he was having trouble .... ⁷ his boss, and he's responsible .... ⁸ a whole team of people. He might just be tired .... ⁹ working so hard. He was really cross .... ¹⁰ his boss for making him work last Saturday: it was his birthday!

JACK   His birthday? Are you sure you're right .... ¹¹ that? I thought it was next week! No wonder he's annoyed .... ¹² me. I forgot his birthday!

E A new job

Complete Kasia's email to her friend, Andy, using the prepositional phrases from the box.

> advice on   at home   by bike   different from   effect on   happy about
> interested in   into town   on holiday   on the corner   on the way
> polite to   ready for   reason for   responsible for

Hi Andy,

I tried to ring you yesterday, but you weren't ...._at home_........ ⁰. Did you go .... ¹ with Gemma? I remember you saying that you were .... ² that new Italian film.

Well, the .... ³ this message is to tell you about my first day at my new job. It's very .... ⁴ my old one. I was .... ⁵ a lot of hard work on my first day, and didn't know how welcoming the people would be, but everyone was very .... ⁶ me and very friendly. The office is .... ⁷ of Prince Street and I'm really .... ⁸ the fact that I can get there .... ⁹. I'm sure cycling every day will have a good .... ¹⁰ me - I have to cycle up a big hill .... ¹¹ there, so I'm hoping to get fit!

I'm going to be .... ¹² all the new customers, and my boss has offered to give me some .... ¹³ how to keep them happy! I'll let you know how the week has gone on Saturday, before you go .... ¹⁴ to France.

Bye for now,

Kasia

OVER TO YOU   Now go to page 125.

25 Prepositions (2)
Preposition + noun + preposition

1 Some prepositional phrases have the form **preposition + noun + preposition**:

preposition	noun	preposition
at	the beginning	of
in	love	with
with	regard	to

2 We can use these phrases to talk about the position of something:

> at the back of   at the bottom of
> at the front of   at the top of   in front of
> in the middle of   on top of

> I found an empty seat **at the back of** the hall.
> Mary sits **in front of** me.
> The remote control is **on top of** the TV.

3 We can also use **prepositional phrases** to explain the order that things happen in:

> at the beginning of   in the middle of
> at the end of

> **At the end of** his talk he thanked his co-workers.
> Some people walked out **in the middle of** the show.

4 Other common **prepositional phrases** with this form include:

> as a result of   on the point of   by means of
> in case of   in charge of   in favour of
> on behalf of   in sight of   in spite of
> in touch with   in contact with   in love with
> with regard to   in addition to

> *In case of* fire, break the glass. (= If there is a fire, break the glass.)
> I keep **in touch with** them by email. (= communicate)
> I think Jim's **in love with** his boss.

Grammar in action

1 We can use **prepositional phrases** to say where things are. Here, we're describing a classroom:
> Jamie sits at the back of the classroom, just in front of the bookshelf.
> The whiteboard is at the front of the class and the teacher always writes the date in the middle of it.

2 We can use **prepositional phrases** to describe the order that things happen in books we've read or films we've seen:
> The main character appears at the beginning of the first chapter. At first, she seems just an ordinary woman, but in the end we realize how much she has changed. In fact, at the end of the book she has become a real celebrity.

3 We can use **prepositional phrases** in formal letters:
> With regard to your application, I am pleased to inform you that we'd like to offer you the job.
> The company is in favour of letting you work from home but you must keep in contact with us.
> In addition to your normal work, we will ask you to be in charge of organizing the Christmas party.

A Saying where things are

Look at this picture of Aisha's classroom. Complete this description of it by writing a prepositional phrase in each space.

<u>At the back of</u> ⁰ the classroom there is a projector. Aisha's desk is .... ¹ the room. Colin is sitting .... ² her. The teacher has written 'Homework' .... ³ the board. There is a TV .... ⁴ the classroom and the class mascot, Timmy, is .... ⁵ the television.

B Writing a formal letter

A journalist has written a letter asking to visit a new factory. In the reply below, put one of the prepositional phrases from the box in each space.

> at the bottom of   in case   in line with   in touch with
> in view of   on behalf of   ~~with regard to~~

Dear Ms. Turnbull,

Thank you for your recent letter. _With regard to_ [0] your request to visit our new automatic factory, I would like to suggest Monday 7 March, when there will be a guided visit for journalists. .... [1] company policy, you will not be allowed to take photographs. However, you may carry a mobile phone .... [2] somebody needs to get .... [3] you. If you accept the proposed date and these conditions, please fill in the form .... [4] this page and return it to me as soon as possible. Please note that .... [5] the large number of requests that we receive, the next possible date that we could offer after this would not be until October. .... [6] the management team, I look forward to welcoming you.

Yours sincerely,

Sean Preston

PR Manager

C Talking about a film you've seen

Complete this film review by circling the correct prepositional phrases each time.

At the beginning of / In front of [0] the film we meet Sara, a young teacher who is in contact with / in charge of / in addition to [1] the activities at a sports centre during the week. In case of / As a result of / At the top of [2] extra demand at the weekend, the boss asks her to work on Saturday in sight of / on behalf of / on top of [3] her normal hours. She doesn't really want to do any more hours so at first / at the end of / in the middle of [4] she says no. But after thinking about it, she offers to work on Saturday in case of / in return for / with regard to [5] a day off during the week. The boss doesn't immediately accept the idea but at the back of / in the end / on the point of [6] he agrees. On Saturday evening she has to give a yoga class; all the students are women except one man at the beginning of / in the middle of / at the end of [7] the room. After the class, the young man is the last to leave. 'My name's Rick,' he says to Sara. 'I've often seen you here at the gym and I've finally got a chance to speak to you.' Well, they start going out together and soon they fall in love with / in spite of / in contact with [8] each other, so Sara is glad that she decided to work on Saturday. The story follows their developing romance and at the end of / on behalf of / in touch with [9] the film we hear wedding bells, but we don't actually see them get married.

5 We can use some **prepositional phrases** to link a statement with what we have just said or what we are going to say:

*Don't forget to water the flowers, **in particular** my beautiful roses.* (= Please take special care of my roses.)

*Polar bears are in danger **because of** climate change.*

Grammar in action

4 We can use some **prepositional phrases** to give extra information or examples to support what we are saying:

> for example   in fact   in particular

A teacher might use these phrases in the classroom:

Remember to use the word 'please' when making a request. For example, 'Could you shut the window please?' It's very important, in particular when speaking to people you don't know.

5 We use some prepositional phrases to give a summary or a conclusion about what we have said before:

> in other words   in brief/short   in conclusion

These are useful when explaining our opinions in a formal situation, like a presentation:

We must do something now to protect the environment. In other words, now is the time for us to protect the rainforests. In short, it is our responsibility to stop global warming.

6 We use some **prepositional phrases** to explain or give reasons for things:

> because of   thanks to   due to

We might try to explain our bad luck:

Thanks to the terrible weather, I was completely wet when I arrived at the station. And then the trains were running late because of a tree that had fallen on the line.

(For more information on **because**, see p. 102.)

7 Some **prepositional phrases** are connected with time:

> at night   in the morning/afternoon/evening
> in time (= not late)   on time (= at the agreed
> time)   in a hurry/rush   in the meantime

He was in a hurry and didn't want to be late, so he ran to make sure he arrived on time.

D   Which preposition?

Cross out the incorrect preposition in each of the following sentences.

0 I don't like to go out *in/at* night.

1 Because *of/for* an engine problem, I had to take my car to the garage.

2 Dad always leaves work early on Fridays so he can be home *at/in* time for dinner.

3 The aeroplane had to make an emergency landing at Heathrow due *to/for* a technical problem.

4 I usually have a cup of tea *in/on* the afternoon.

5 Jeff wasn't hurt in the car accident, thanks *for/to* his seatbelt.

E Lost in the forest

Tom and Ann are on a walking holiday. Complete their conversation using the prepositional phrases from the box.

> in a hurry   ~~in other words~~   in the meantime
> at night   for example   thanks to   in fact

TOM   I'm sorry, Ann, I really don't know where we are.

ANN   So, _in other words_ ⁰ , we're lost.

TOM   Yes. _____ ¹, I don't think we're going to find the youth hostel before it gets dark.

ANN   But there might be wild animals out here, _____ ² bears and wolves - I don't want to be out in the forest _____ ³.

TOM   Neither do I, so we'll keep walking for now. But _____ ⁴, we should look out for a good place to put up the tent, just in case.

ANN   Erm, the tent?

TOM   Don't tell me you forgot to bring the tent! So, _____ ⁵ you, we have nowhere to sleep tonight!

ANN   Well, I forgot it because you were _____ ⁶ to leave this morning.

F News reports

Complete these extracts from TV news reports using the prepositional phrases from the box.

> on time   ~~in particular~~   in conclusion   in the morning   due to

0 Crime rates in the capital are rising. _In particular_ ⁰ , car theft has increased by 75%.

1 Fuel resources are running out, the cost of petrol is rising, and industry is polluting the atmosphere. _____ ¹ , we need to find alternative sources of energy.

2 _____ ² the gradual increase in the price of meat, more and more people are becoming vegetarian.

3 Last month, Western Rail announced that over 90% of its trains arrived at their destinations _____ ³ .

4 Over 30% of people admitted that they have difficulty getting out of bed _____ ⁴ .

OVER TO YOU Now go to page 125.

26 Linking words
Either … or, neither … nor, both … and, because, for

1 We use **either … or** to talk about alternatives:
*You can pay **either** when you order the books **or** when they are delivered.*

2 We use **neither … nor** (= not one and not the other) when we want to show that a negative statement is true of two things:
***Neither** the managers **nor** the workers have changed their opinion.*

3 We use **both … and** to emphasize that two ideas or two things go together:
*Sally is **both** the club secretary **and** the team captain.*
*The price includes **both** transport **and** the entrance ticket.*

(For more information on **either** and **neither**, see p. 91.)

4 We use **because** to explain the cause or reason for something:
*Why were you late? ~ **Because** there was a traffic jam.*
*Sally went to bed **because** she was exhausted.*

When a noun expresses the cause, we use **because of**:
*Why were you late? ~ **Because** of a traffic jam.*

(For more information on **because of**, see p. 100.)

5 We can use **for** + **noun** to talk about why we do something and **for** + *-ing* form to explain the purpose of something:
*Sean went to the shops **for a newspaper**.*
*What is it for? ~ It's **for slicing** cheese.*

Grammar in action

1 We can use **either … or** when there are two options and we need to make a choice. For example, when we are choosing a holiday:
I'd like to stay either at The Regal or at The Pacific.
~ The Pacific is very popular– a wonderful choice. ~
Does the hotel have double beds? ~ You can have either a double bed or single bed.

2 We use **neither … nor** to explain that two choices are not available:
I'm afraid that neither the library nor the swimming pool are open at the moment.

> Notice that we use a positive verb with **neither … nor**.
> *Neither the supermarket **nor** the baker's have any cakes left.*

3 We use **both … and** when we want to say that two things are necessary, or to emphasize that two things are included in a price or offer:
My son needs both his maths books and his football things today.
The price includes both lunch and dinner.

4 We can use **because** to explain why people or things are (not) where they should be, especially in answer to a question with **why**:
Why aren't Jack and Julie here today? ~ Because he's at a conference and Julie's away all week because she's had an operation.

5 We can use **for** to talk about the purpose of something, or to explain why we do something.
This knife is used for cutting steak. ~ Are we having steak for dinner? That's expensive! ~ Well, Claire's won a prize for poetry at school, so we're having steak for dinner to celebrate.

A Travel options

Use *both … and*, *either … or* or *neither … nor* to complete these sentences about the hotel rooms.

		shower	bath	radio	TV
Deluxe Rooms	The Grosvenor Suite	✓	✓	✓	✓
	The Longford Suite	✓	✓	✓	✓
Standard Rooms	The Mercator Suite	✓	✗	✗	✓
	The Hirst Suite	✗	✓	✓	✗
Economy Rooms	The Essex Suite	✗	✗	✗	✗
	The Croydon Suite	✗	✗	✗	✗

0 A deluxe room has ___both___ a shower ___and___ a bath.

1 A standard room has _____ a shower _____ a bath.

2 An economy room has _____ a shower _____ a bath.

3 A deluxe room has _____ a radio _____ a TV.

4 A standard room has _____ a radio _____ a TV.

5 An economy room doesn't have _____ a radio _____ a TV.

B A passport application

Frank is talking to his younger brother about his passport application. Complete the dialogue with *either … or*, *neither … nor*, *both … and*, *because*, or *for*.

FRANK I've just completed my passport application.

JIMMY I thought you had a passport. Why do you want a new one?

FRANK ___Because___ [0] I want to go to America, and my old passport isn't digital. To go to the States, you've got to have _____ [1] a digital passport _____ [2] a visa, and it's easier to get a passport than a visa. Now I need a responsible adult to witness my application.

FRANK I'll sign it for you.

FRANK Come on, Jimmy. You're _____ [3] responsible _____ [4] an adult.

JIMMY That's not fair.

FRANK Well, you're only 15, and you're always getting into trouble _____ [5] telling lies.

JIMMY Oh, all right. What about Mum and Dad? I suppose you'd accept them as _____ [6] responsible _____ [7] adult.

FRANK Of course, but they're no good precisely _____ [8] they're my parents. The form says that the witness can't be _____ [9] a relative _____ [10] a friend. I think I'll ask Mrs Briggs. She's a bank manager.

JIMMY Why her?

FRANK Well, _____ [11] she's a bank manager, she must be the sort of responsible person they want.

JIMMY You don't usually say nice things about bank people.

FRANK That's _____ [12] they always complain when I'm overdrawn.

Linking words
In order to, so that, such a

6 Purpose

We use (**in order**) **to** + **verb** to express the reason for doing something. **In order to** is more formal than **to**. The verb after **to** must refer to the subject of the sentence:

> *Paul has stopped playing tennis (**in order**) **to** spend more time with his family.* (= Paul wants more time …)
> *Kate phoned the station (**in order**) **to** find out the times of the trains.* (= Kate wanted to find out …)

(**In order**) **to** can also come first:

> (**In order**) **to** *find out the times of the trains, Kate phoned the station.*

The negative is **in order not to**:

> *I took a taxi **in order not to** be late.*

7 We use **so** (**that**) + **a statement** to explain why somebody has done something. The purpose usually goes at the end:

> *Paul has stopped playing tennis **so** (**that**) he has more time for his family.*

The subject of the clause after **so** does not need to be the same as the subject in the first part of the sentence:

> ***Jack** put sunscreen on the children **so** (**that**) **the sun** wouldn't burn them.*

8 We use **so** + **adjective/adverb** + (**that**) to explain the consequences or results of a situation:

> *It was **so cold** (**that**) we all had to put on extra clothes.*
> *The salad was **so delicious** (**that**) I asked for more!*

9 We can also use **so** with **much**, **little**, **many** and **few** (+ **noun**):

> *There was **so much** snow they couldn't get the car out.*
> *Gary's eaten **so many** apples (**that**) he feels sick.*

10 We can also use **such** (**a**) (+ **adjective**) + noun to express the consequences or results of a situation:

> *It was **such an awful film** (**that**) most people left before the end.*

> **So** and **such**, without the result of a situation, make the adjectives or nouns they accompany stronger:
> > *I'm **so** hungry!* (stronger than *I'm hungry.*)
> > *He's **such** an unfriendly man.* (stronger than *He's an unfriendly man.*)

Grammar in action

⑥ We use (**in order**) **to** to explain a particular reason for an action, for example when we say why someone has made changes to their normal routine:

> *My dad's getting up earlier these days in order to do some exercise before he goes to work. He's also trying to come home earlier to help us with our homework.*

⑦ We can use **so** (**that**) to explain our reasons for making changes:

> *Granny is coming to stay for a few days. Alex can move in with Peter so (that) Granny can have a bedroom for herself. We'll have to keep her door closed so (that) the dog doesn't wake her in the morning.*

⑧ We can use **so … that** and **such … that** to explain the results of a situation. This can also explain why we have done something. Here, we are talking about what happened on a holiday:

> *We found Venice so expensive that we only stayed for two days. We were in such a rush to see everything that we had to miss some of the most famous sights.*

C   Holiday problems

Read the email that Jane sent to a friend about the things that went wrong with her holiday. Complete the sentences with *so … that* and *such … that*.

Hi Kelly,

We just got back yesterday, and you wouldn't believe all the things that went wrong!

Firstly, the children couldn't go sailing because there was a very strong wind.

0 The wind was _so strong that_ the children couldn't go sailing.

0 There was _such a strong wind that_ the children couldn't go sailing.

In the evening, we had to queue for the restaurant because there were a lot of people.

1 In the evening there were .... we had to queue for the restaurant.

We couldn't go out because it was very cold.

2 It was .... we couldn't go out.

My cousins moved to another hotel because there was a lot of noise.

3 There was .... my cousins moved to another hotel.

We stayed in the shade because it was a very hot day.

4 It was .... we had to stay in the shade.

5 The day was .... we had to stay in the shade.

Jim couldn't go on the last excursion because he had very little money left.

6 Jim had .... he couldn't go on the last excursion.

And worst of all, we had to drink lots of water because the food was very salty.

7 And worst of all, the food was .... we had to drink lots of water.

8 And worst of all, it was .... we had to drink lots of water.

Apart from that, we had a wonderful time!

Jane

D Moving abroad

Complete the following conversation by adding words or phrases from the box.

and	because	because	because	both	either	for
in order to	in order to	or	so much that	so that	such	such

MIA   My sister and her husband are thinking of moving to Canada.
....*because*....⁰ they can't find decent jobs in Britain.

MATT Your sister's well qualified, isn't she?

MIA   Yes, after school she spent a year abroad ....¹ learn a couple of languages, and at university she studied ....² she never had time to come home. That didn't please my parents, of course.

MATT Why not?

MIA   ....³ they paid all her expenses ....⁴ she didn't need to take part-time jobs, thinking that she would spend more time at home. But she got a good degree. She even won a prize ....⁵ her final project.

MATT And what about her husband?

MIA   Well, he's got ....⁶ a degree ....⁷ several years' experience, but he's been out of work for almost six months. He says it's ....⁸ a long time since he worked that he's almost forgotten what it's like. He's applied for several jobs, but apparently he hasn't been offered ....⁹ a permanent contract ....¹⁰ even a decent salary. And ....¹¹ he's well qualified, he refuses to accept poor conditions.

MATT Are they going to go to Canada together?

MIA   No, he's going first ....¹² find somewhere to live.

MATT Well, I hope they do very well, but I think it's ....¹³ a pity that young people have to go abroad to find work.

OVER TO YOU Now go to page 125.

1 We can make a **negative zero** or **first conditional sentence** by using **if … not** or **unless**:

> They'll miss the train **if** they **don't** leave at once.
> They'll miss the train **unless** they leave at once.

Notice that the clause with **unless** usually goes in second position.

(For more information on zero and first conditionals, see p. 58.)

2 We use **in case** to join two sentences together when we want to explain the reason for doing something, or when we want to avoid a possible problem later:

> We've bought some extra meat **in case** my sister and her husband turn up. (= because they might turn up)
> Take your passport **in case** you need to prove your identity. (= because you might need to prove your identity)

> We do not use **will** after **unless** or **in case**.
> To talk about the future we use a present tense:
> > I'll make an extra cake **in case Jane brings** the children too.
> > I can't come to your party at the weekend **unless I find** a babysitter.

3 We can also use **moreover**, **furthermore** or **what's more** to connect two statements. The second statement adds more information related to the first:

> The local sports complex has excellent facilities.
> **Moreover/Furthermore/What's more**, it is open seven days a week.

Grammar in action

1 We can use **if … not** or **unless** to say what will happen if we don't do something, for example when we are talking about a business contract:

> I won't consider a new contract if they don't pay for the previous delivery. ~ But they refuse to pay unless we give them a discount on two items that they say were damaged.

2 We can use **in case** to explain the arrangements and plans that have been made for an event, for example for a school sports day:

> We've ordered two big tents for the parents in case it rains, and there'll be a doctor and a nurse on hand in case we have any injuries.

3 We often use **furthermore**, **moreover**, and **what's more** in business letters, formal speeches or when writing to a newspaper:

> Furthermore, I would like to draw your attention to the last paragraph of the article.

A In case or unless?

Complete these sentences by crossing out *in case* or *unless*.

0 I'll bring an umbrella *in case / unless* it rains.

1 I won't bring an umbrella *in case / unless* it rains.

2 You should always wear a seatbelt *in case / unless* you have an accident while driving.

3 I don't usually wear glasses *in case / unless* I'm driving.

4 You'll catch a cold *in case / unless* you wear a coat.

5 I'm leaving this company *in case / unless* I get a pay rise.

B   Business conditions

Read these business conditions and rewrite them using the words given.

0   We cannot deliver before Christmas if the order is not received by 30 November.
We cannot deliver before Christmas unless *the order is received by 30 November* .

1   If the boxes are not kept in a dry place, the company cannot accept responsibility.
The company cannot accept responsibility unless ....

2   We cannot offer a refund unless the goods are in perfect condition.
If ...., we cannot offer a refund.

3   If we do not hear from you within a week, we will take legal action.
We will take legal action unless ....

4   We will not accept returned items which are not in good condition.
We will not accept items unless ....

5   Customers cannot visit the showroom without an appointment.
If ...., they cannot visit the showroom.

C   Explaining plans and arrangements

Read these short conversations and rewrite the sentences using *in case*.

0   There was a chance that my sister would visit. So I didn't go out.
I didn't go out *in case my sister visited* .

1   I thought my husband might wonder where I was, so I phoned him.
I phoned ....

2   It might rain later, so you should take an umbrella.
Take ....

3   You should write down the name of the film, so you don't forget it.
Write ....

4   Tina might come for dinner, so we'll buy some more food.
We'll buy ....

5   It's possible you won't be able to find the hotel, so I'll draw you a map.
I'll draw ....

4 We can use **but** and **although** to join two sentences together when we want to express a contrast between two statements or ideas:

> *Sheffield used to be a very dirty city, **but** now it's much cleaner.*
> ***Although** it's a simple camera, it's very expensive.*

But always goes in the middle of the sentence.
Although can go in the middle or at the beginning.

Though means the same as **although**, but is is less formal.

> ***Though** Tom has a reputation for being difficult, he's helped me a lot.*

We can also use **though** at the end of the sentence:

> *Tom has a reputation for being difficult. He's helped me a lot, **though**.*

5 We use **however** in more formal situations to emphasize the contrast between two sentences; **however** is separated with commas:

> *John's written work is the best in the class. His drawing, **however**, is very poor. / **However**, his drawing is very poor.*

6 We can use **on the other hand** to express a contrast; **on the other hand** is separated with commas:

> *John's written work is the best in the class. His drawing, **on the other hand**, is very poor.*

7 We sometimes use **on the one hand** together with **on the other hand**:

> ***On the one hand**, the campsite is well run and has good services. **On the other hand**, it is quite a long way from the sea.*

Grammar in action

④ We can use these expressions in formal situations, to make comments on a situation. This might be when we write a report about someone's work:

> *Sally was taken on last year as a trainee illustrator, but now she has a permanent contract. Although she has not worked here for very long, she has gained the respect of her colleagues. She still has things to improve in her hand drawing. On the other hand, her computer creations are very amusing.*

⑤ We can also use these expressions to give personal opinions and views about proposals or changes, for example to talk about changes to a town centre:

> *In general, I agree that the town centre has to change, but I'm not convinced by the present proposal. It argues that traffic should be banned completely, which is fine for younger people. Elderly people will find it difficult to get to the shops, though.*

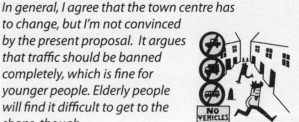

D   Making comments about people's work

Read these comments about five new members of staff in a company. Rewrite the sentences using the word given. You may need to change the punctuation.

Sally Brown

Sally works hard. She is not very productive.

0 although: *Although Sally works hard, she is not very productive.*

0 but: *Sally works hard but she is not very productive.*

0 however: *Sally works hard. However, she is not very productive.*

Brian Shepherdson

Brian is quite young. His work is greatly appreciated.

1 although: ....

2 however: ....

Mary Martin

Mary is a favourite with the boss. Her colleagues don't like her.

3 but: ....

4 although: ....

5 however: ....

Joan de la Forest

Joan's English is not very good. She gets her message across.

6 however: ....

7 though: ....

Tony Kelly

Tony always arrives late. He usually finishes his work on time.

8 but: ....

9 although: ....

WORD FOCUS

What is the correct definition of *to get one's message across*?

A to send an email

B to make oneself understood

E Town plans

Phil and Eve are talking about proposed changes to their town. Complete their conversation by choosing the right expression.

PHIL I've read about the plans in the newspaper *but/however* ⁰ I haven't read the actual proposal.

EVE It all seems quite sensible to me. *What's more/On the other hand* ¹, the proposal has the support of all the political parties. If you go to the town hall, you can read the proposal free. *Although/However* ², if you want to have your own copy, you have to pay for it. One of the main things is that all cars will be banned from the town centre *unless/if* ³ they have special permission.

PHIL I like the idea of a pedestrian shopping area in the centre of town. It'll be difficult if you have heavy things to carry, *though/but* ⁴.

EVE During shopping hours, there'll be a free electric bus service so you won't need to walk very far. *However/Moreover* ⁵, the big shops will have extra staff *in case/unless* ⁶ anyone needs help with their shopping bags.

PHIL I've read that there'll be a big underground car park.

EVE Yes, but there are in fact two ways to get to town from the suburbs. You can drive in and park underground, *if/though* ⁷ that will be pretty expensive. *On the other hand/Furthermore* ⁸, you can park your car near a bus stop and take the bus into town, which will be cheaper. And *if/unless* ⁹ you don't want to pay each time, you can get a bus pass. *What's more/However* ¹⁰, that only makes sense if you're a regular shopper.

PHIL So the pass isn't free.

EVE No, you have to pay *if/unless* ¹¹ you're disabled or over 60.

PHIL I think I'll send my mother to do the shopping because she's over 60. *What's more/On the other hand* ¹², she loves shopping!

OVER TO YOU **Now go to page 125.**

1 If we use a sentence like:
The man was very helpful.

it may not be clear which man. We can make it clear like this:
*The man **who/that served me** was very helpful.*

Who is a relative pronoun and links the relative clause (**who served me**) to the main clause (**The man was very helpful**).

The relative clause answers the question '**Which person/thing?**'. We call this a defining relative clause and we do not use commas (,):
*The man was very helpful. ~ Which man? ~ The man **who/that served me**.*

2 We use **who** or **that** to refer to people:
*I thanked the woman **who/that helped me**.*

and **which** or **that** to refer to things:
*That's the machine **which/that makes paper**.*

3 **Who**, **which** or **that** can be the subject of the relative clause:

subject		
The girl	*who*	*won* was really happy.
The girl		*won.*
That's the parrot	*that*	*talks!*
The parrot		*talks!*

4 **Who**, **which** or **that** can be the object of the relative clause:

object		
The woman	*who*	*I served* was very rude.
I served	*the woman.*	
They sold the car	*that*	*we wanted.*
We wanted	*the car.*	

> In formal English, we can also use **whom** instead of **who**, when it is the object of the relative clause:
> *The woman **whom I served** was very rude.*

5 When **who**, **which** or **that** is the object, we can leave it out:
The woman I served was rude.
They sold the car we wanted.

6 We use **whose** in place of the possessive adjectives **his**, **her**, **their**, etc.:
*They interviewed a man **whose wife had disappeared**.* (= His wife had disappeared.)
*That's the girl **whose photo was in the paper**.* (= Her photo was in the paper.)

We only use **whose** with people, countries and organizations, not things or ideas.

(For more information on leaving out words in defining relative clauses, see p. 120.)

Grammar in action

1 We use **defining relative clauses** to identify which thing we are talking about. These might be the particular things we need to complete a task:
Can you bring me a hammer? ~ Which one? ~ The one that I bought yesterday. ~ OK. Where is it? ~ It's in a bag that's lying on the kitchen table.

2 We can also use **defining relative clauses** to identify which people we are talking about. This can help to avoid confusion, especially in conversation:
I met Tilly Lott this morning. ~ Who's she? ~ She's the woman who came to the concert with Tony. She's the one that I spoke to in the interval.

A Who's who?

Look at the table with information about two couples. Complete the sentences with a relative pronoun.

	work	hobby	spouse	spouse's work
Cath	teacher	reading	Ben	postman
John	taxi driver	cycling	Jane	nurse
Toby	cook	jogging	Jenny	waitress
Sally	bus driver	photography	Dave	mechanic

0 Cath is the woman ___who/that___ is married to Ben.

1 John is the taxi driver _____ Jane is married to.

2 Jenny is the woman _____ husband likes jogging.

3 Dave is the man _____ works as a mechanic.

4 Cycling is the hobby _____ John likes best.

5 Ben is married to a woman _____ hobby is reading.

6 Jogging is something _____ Toby likes to do.

7 The man _____ brings the post is called Ben.

8 Photography is something _____ interests Sally.

9 Sally is the woman _____ works as a bus driver.

10 Reading is a hobby _____ Cath enjoys.

B Identifying people and things

Here are some sentences found in a lifestyle magazine. Combine the two sentences in two ways, using the words given.

> They interviewed the player. She had won the competition.

0 The player _who they interviewed_ had won the competition.

0 They interviewed the player _who had won_ the competition.

> My cousin bought a car. It cost £20,000.

1 My cousin bought a car _____ £20,000.

2 The car _____ cost £20,000.

> The parents of the young man were refugees. My sister works with him

3 The parents of the young man _____ my sister were refugees.

4 My sister works with a young man _____ refugees.

> Thieves burgled a house. The owners were on holiday.

5 The owners of the house _____ were on holiday.

6 The owners _____ were on holiday.

> A woman saved a child from drowning. Her photo was in the paper.

7 The paper had a photo of the woman _____ from drowning.

8 The woman _____ in the paper saved a child from drowning.

Spouse is the formal or legal word for 'husband' or 'wife'.

WORD FOCUS

7 Look at these sentences:

Melanie works in the hairdresser's.

*Melanie, **who lives next door to me**, works in the hairdresser's.*

Here the relative clause (**who lives next door to me**) adds extra information, but is not necessary for us to identify Melanie. We can understand the first sentence without this extra information. **Who lives next door to me** is a non-defining relative clause and we use commas (,) to separate it from the rest of the sentence.

8 **Who** and **which** can be the subject of the relative clause:

*Tony Blair, **who was Prime Minister for 10 years**, studied law at Oxford University.*

*The Prime Minister lives at 10 Downing Street, **which is in London**.*

9 **Who** and **which** can also be the object of the relative clause. When **who** is the object, we can also use **whom**:

*There were many stories about Jack Jones, **who/whom** many people suspected of the crime.*

*The severe thunderstorms, **which** nobody had forecast, caused floods in several places.*

10 We use **whose** in place of the possessive adjectives **his, her, their**, etc.:

*Van Gogh, **whose paintings now sell for millions**, hardly managed to sell any during his lifetime.*

11 Compare the two sentences:

*Sara lent Jim her camera, **which** was practically new.*
(*which* = her camera)
*Sara lent Jim her camera, **which** was very kind.*

(*which* = the fact that Sara lent Jim her camera)

We call the second type a 'sentence relative clause' because **which** refers to all of the previous part of the sentence.

Grammar in action

3 We often use **non-defining relative clauses** in formal writing. They are common in news reports, and biographies, e.g.:

Tony Blair, whose full name is Anthony Charles Lynton Blair, was born in 1953. In 1980 he married Cherie Booth, whom he had met in 1976. From 1994 he was the leader of the Labour Party, which won three consecutive elections.

4 We can also use **non-defining relative clauses** in descriptions of places, for example in guide books and travel articles, e.g.:

Venice, which is very popular with tourists, lies on the Adriatic Sea. The town is crossed by many canals, which are used for the transport of both people and goods. The main canal is the Grand Canal, which is lined with dozens of fine buildings.

5 We can use **sentence relative clauses** to give a reaction to, or comment on, facts, e.g.:

My grandmother walks everywhere, which is very good for her health.
Simon and Sandra never wanted to have children, which surprised some of their friends.

C   Giving information about well-known people

Here is some information from a website about well-known people. Make one sentence from the notes given, making the underlined parts into relative clauses.

0   Bill Clinton <u>was US President from 1993 to 2001</u>. He was born in Hope. <u>It is a small town in Arkansas.</u>

Bill Clinton, who was US President from 1993 to 2001, was born in Hope, which is a small town in Arkansas.

1   Virginia Woolf. <u>Her sister was a painter</u>. She wrote *A Room of One's Own*. <u>The book deals with the difficulties for women in a man's world.</u>

....

....

2 In 1958 Rosalind Franklin died of cancer. <u>She helped to discover the structure of DNA.</u> <u>In those days cancer was incurable.</u>

....

....

3 Grantham <u>lies in Lincolnshire.</u> It is famous as the birthplace of Margaret Thatcher. <u>She was British Prime Minister for 11 years.</u>

....

....

4 'Imagine' <u>is still a very popular song.</u> It was written by John Lennon. <u>He died in 1980.</u>

....

....

D   Comments on facts or things?

Underline the words that *which* refers to.

0 They spent whole afternoons in <u>the garden</u>, which lay behind the house.

0 <u>Brian was in the army for 9 years</u>, which explains his respect for discipline.

1 Sara read *War and Peace* in just two weeks, which is probably a record.

2 Denis let me borrow his car, which is practically new.

3 We often visit the Lake District, which is very good for hiking.

4 The manager accused Bill of stealing, which almost led to a strike.

E   Frida Kahlo

Complete the text by writing in relative pronouns and including a comma if one is necessary.

The artist Frida Kahlo, ... *who* .... [0] died in 1954, is becoming more and more popular. As a child she suffered from polio .... [1] left her right leg thinner than her left. She disguised this by wearing skirts .... [2] reached to her ankles. She had several sisters but was closest to her father .... [3] encouraged her to study medicine. One day when she was 18, a bus .... [4] she was travelling in was hit by a car. In the accident she broke several bones, including some in her back. These injuries .... [5] resulted in many operations, affected her for the rest of her life. She left her medical studies to paint, and sought advice from Diego Garcia .... [6] paintings she very much admired. Garcia encouraged her, and later they got married .... [7] didn't please Frida's family. Her paintings .... [8] were often self-portraits, were painted in a style .... [9] was influenced by popular Mexican art. During her lifetime she was considered less important than her husband but today she receives the recognition .... [10] she deserves.

OVER TO YOU   Now go to page 125.

29 Expressions of time, place, and reason
When, while, until, before, after, as soon as

1 We can use **when** to relate two events in time. We can form sentences with **when** like this:

> clause + when + clause
> when + clause + clause

The verb after **when** is normally in the past simple or present simple:

> *I was having a shower **when** the phone **rang**.*
> ***When** the rain **started**, we went inside the house.*

2 We can also use **while** to relate two events in time, where one of the events is still in progress. We use the same patterns as **when** but the verb after **while** is normally either **be** or a continuous tense because it refers to an action that is unfinished at the time:

> *Can you buy me a magazine **while** you're in town?*
> ***While** I **was having** a shower, the phone rang.*

3 We can use **until** or **till** with a time phrase or a statement to set a time limit:

> *We're staying **until/till next Friday**. (= we leave next Friday)*
> *They sat under the tree **until/till it got dark**.*

4 We use **before** and **after** with a phrase or a statement to talk about the order of events:

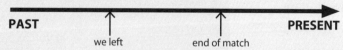

PAST   we left   end of match   PRESENT

> *The match finished **after we had left**.*

5 We can use **as soon as** to relate two events in time, one immediately after the other:

> ***As soon as** she finished her exams, she went abroad.*

6 When a sentence has two parts that refer to the future, we use the present simple after **when**, **before**, **after**, **as soon as** and **until**. We use **will** or **be going to** in the other part of the sentence:

> *What are you going to do **when** you **finish** your exams?*
> ***After** Jenny **arrives**, we'll go for dinner.*
> *Your guide will contact you **as soon as** you **arrive** at the hotel.*

> When these expressions are at the beginning of the sentence, there is usually a comma, but not when they are at the end:
> > ***While** I was having a shower, the phone rang.*
> > *The phone rang **while** I was having a shower.*

7 We use **by** with a time or date to mean 'at the latest', or before a certain time:

> *I want you to be home **by 10 o' clock**.*
> *(= not later than 10 o'clock)*

Grammar in action

1 We can use these time expressions to explain events and the order they happen in. We might tell a story about events in the past:

> *While I was shopping yesterday, I saw a man steal a handbag. When he noticed that I was looking at him, he started to run, but before he got out of the shop, he fell and dropped the bag.*

2 We can also use these expressions to explain the order of tasks in a recipe or instructions for making something:

> *Remember, before you start, you must always read the instructions carefully. As soon as you open the box, lay all the pieces on the floor. Put the pieces together in order until the cupboard is finished.*

A Family matters

Look at what happened to Maria on Monday. Write complete sentences using past tenses and the word in brackets.

Breakfast: 8.05–8.20; teeth: 8.25–8.30; phone: 8.15

She / have / breakfast / she / clean / her teeth (before)

0 *She had breakfast before she cleaned her teeth.*

She / have / breakfast / the phone / ring / (while)

0 *While she was having breakfast, the phone rang.*

School: any time before 8.45; History lesson: 10.00; basketball match: 12.00; home: 4.30

She / arrive / school / 8.45 (by)

1 ....

She / play / basketball / history lesson (after)

2 ....

She / not / get home / 4.30 (until)

3 ....

Homework: 4.45–5.30; television: 5.30–6.20; mother come home: 5.55

Maria / finish / her homework / she / watch / television (after)

4 ....

She / watch / television / her mother / come / home (when)

5 ....

Father wash the dishes: 9.50–10.15; brother tell jokes: 9.55; father go to bed: 10.20

Her brother / tell / a couple of jokes / her father / wash / the dishes (while)

6 ....

Her father / go / to bed / he / wash / the dishes (after)

7 ....

B Cooking instructions

Read this recipe and complete the cooking instructions by circling the correct word.

Cheese omelette

Break two eggs into a bowl. • *By / Before / While* [0] you beat the eggs, make sure that there are no bits of shell. • Add a pinch of salt and beat the eggs *until / as soon as / while* [1] they are completely mixed. • *Until / While / After* [2] you have grated the cheese, add it to the mixture. • Heat some oil in a frying pan and *as soon as / until / by* [3] it is hot, pour in the mixture. • Stir the mixture gently *before / while / after* [4] it is cooking *by / after / until* [5] it is almost set. • Then fold it in half and *when / while / by* [6] it is golden brown on both sides, turn it onto a plate.

8 We can use **when**, **where** and **why** to emphasize a time, place or reason:

> *Lily went to see Henry on Friday.*
> *Friday was the day **when** Lily went to see Henry.*

> *Tom works at The Wild Duck.*
> *The Wild Duck is the restaurant **where** Tom works.*

> *Pete went to town to buy Dan's birthday present.*
> *The reason **why** Pete went to town was to buy Dan's birthday present.*

9 We use **whenever** to mean 'at any time when' and **wherever** to mean '(at) any place where':

> ***Whenever** I see him, he asks how you are.*
> (= Every time I see him …)
> *The manager will see us **whenever** we want.*
> (= at any time we choose)
> ***Wherever** you find water, there are always plants.*
> (= every place)
> *These days you can take out money **wherever** you are.* (= in any place)

Grammar in action

3 We can use **when**, **where** and **why** to explain which times, places, and reasons we are talking about, for example in a news report:

> *The police have located the house where the car thieves were living, but so far they do not know the reason why they left the stolen cars in the garage.*

4 We can use **whenever** if the time when something happens is not important. For example, when we want to speak to, or meet, someone:

> *Give me a ring whenever you feel like coming round.*

5 We can also use **whenever** to mean 'every time that'. We might want to emphasize the repetition of a bad experience:

> *Whenever we go to that restaurant, I always feel ill the next day.*

6 We use **wherever** when an exact place is not important. It can mean 'anywhere':

> *Sit wherever you like.*

or 'everywhere':

> *It rained wherever we went this summer.*

C   Reporting a crime

Read this newspaper article. Complete the sentences using *when*, *where* or *why*.

Bomb makers escape police

The police have located the house ....<u>where</u>........ ⁰ the bombers were living. However, they arrived ....¹ the house was empty. They said that they found clues to the location of the factory ....² the materials were bought. They have searched the rooms, including the bedrooms ....³ the bombers slept. They think that Friday was the day ....⁴ the bombers abandoned the house. The police are now trying to work out ....⁵ the bombers left in such a hurry and where they are now.

D   Planning a party

Anna is writing to her friend Tom about her party. Complete her email using *when*, *where*, *why*, *whenever* or *wherever*.

Hi Tom

I hope you're well. I'm writing to answer your questions about the party tomorrow evening. The reason ....*why*.... ⁰ we're having the party is to celebrate the end of the exams. It was Friday evening .... ¹ Jenny and I decided to organize something - she had just got back from Vito's (you know, the Italian restaurant .... ² she works) and she had seen some people she knows from college. They were having a special meal because their exams had just finished. It's this Wednesday .... ³ I finish, so we thought we would celebrate too!

Thank you for offering to come round a bit early to help prepare everything. Please come .... ⁴ is convenient for you - I'll be at home all day. Could you bring some balloons? When I was in town yesterday, I couldn't find any, ... ⁵ I looked. I think last week's festival might be the reason .... ⁶ there weren't any left in the shops.

Give me a ring .... ⁷ you need to. See you at the party!

Anna

E   Talking about a trip to scout camp

Sam and Tom are talking on the phone about the happy times they spent at scout camp as young boys. Complete their conversation using one of the words in brackets in each space.

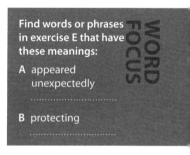

WORD FOCUS

Find words or phrases in exercise E that have these meanings:

A appeared unexpectedly

....

B protecting

....

SAM   Do you remember that place in Devon ....*where*....... ⁰ (where/whenever) we stayed .... ¹ (until/when) we were in the scouts?

TOM   I do. I particularly remember the morning .... ² (when/while) we woke to find our tents surrounded by cows. We went to sleep, but someone forgot to close the gate into the field .... ³ (that/where) the tents were, and the cows wandered in .... ⁴ (while/as soon as) we were sleeping.

SAM   And we couldn't do anything .... ⁵ (until/where) we got them back into the field .... ⁶ (wherever/where) they were supposed to be.

TOM   And do you remember that dog that turned up .... ⁷ (why/whenever) we went swimming in the river? .... ⁸ (As soon as/ Until) we set off from the camp, it appeared from nowhere.

SAM   Yes, it sat by our clothes .... ⁹ (while/before) we were in the water as if it was guarding them.

TOM   I don't think that was the reason .... ¹⁰ (while/why) it waited there. Perhaps it expected us to give it something to eat .... ¹¹ (when/why) we came out of the water.

SAM   I think one or two boys did give it something. But it never came all the way back with us. .... ¹² (When/By) the time we were back at the camp, it had always disappeared.

TOM   I enjoyed those scout camps .... ¹³ (where/wherever) we went, but that stay in Devon was the one I liked the most.

OVER TO YOU   Now go to page 125.

30 Leaving out words
Emma sings and dances.

1 Here are some examples of sentences where we can leave words out, but the meaning is still clear:

> *Molly sings and (she) plays the guitar.*
> *Pigs can't swim but dogs can (swim).*
> *She doesn't want to go but she ought to (go).*

2 When we use **and**, **but**, and **or** to join phrases or longer sentences, we can usually leave out unnecessary words:

> *This machine washes the apples and **it** packs them.*
> → *This machine washes the apples and packs them.*
> *I've cleaned the sitting room and **I've cleaned** my bedroom.*
> → *I've cleaned the sitting room and my bedroom.*
> *Jack seemed nervous but **he seemed** excited.*
> → *Jack seemed nervous but excited.*

3 We can just use an **auxiliary verb** instead of repeating a longer expression:

> *Amy couldn't speak French a year ago, but now she **can**. (= she can speak French)*
> *I thought Tim would get good marks, and he **did**. (= he got good marks)*
> *Who knows the way? ~ I **do**.*

When we use an auxiliary verb in this way, it cannot be a short form:

> *Lucy won't help you but I will. (NOT I'll)*
> *Dan's not coming but Sara is. (NOT Sara's)*

4 With verbs that are usually followed by an infinitive, we can just say **to** instead of completing the phrase:

> *Why don't you talk to him? ~ Because I don't want **to**.*
> *Dave doesn't smoke now but he used **to**.*
> *We'd like to get married but we can't afford **to**.*

Typical verbs include: **have (got)**, **mean**, **plan**, **intend**, **would like**

> We usually miss out **shop**, **house**, **flat**, etc., in expressions such as:
> *I've got to go to the greengrocer's/doctor's.*
> *We're having lunch at my brother's today.*

TIP

Grammar in action

① In conversation, we can leave words out when everyone understands what we are talking about:

> *Can we go to the cinema, Mum? ~ We can if you want to.*

② In formal writing, we leave words out to make what we say more concise (we give only the important and necessary information):

> *If we are asked to provide further information, we will.*

A Office messenger

Donna and Claire are work colleagues. They are using an instant messaging service to arrange a meeting. Cross out the words that can be left out without changing the meaning.

DM Claire – we need to arrange a time and ~~to arrange a~~ place⁰ for tomorrow's meeting.

CP Yes. Well, when are you free?

DM Free from 11 to 12¹.

CP I'm busy till 11.30 – I've got an appointment at the doctor's surgery².

DM Oh. I hope everything's OK. Let's say 11.30 then.

CP Remember that Tony only works mornings and he will have to³ leave by 12.

DM That's OK. We can talk about his parts of the project first, if we have to talk about them first⁴.

CP Good idea. Now, shall I lead the meeting or would you like to lead the meeting⁵?

DM I will lead the meeting⁶. It's my turn. But please can you book a room, and can you send⁷ a reminder to Jim and send an update⁸ to Jeff.

CP Yes, I can do.⁹ Also, I'll order some tea and I'll order some coffee¹⁰.

DM Great, thanks Claire. Ciao. 😃

B Film review

Here is a recent film review. Rewrite the underlined phrases in the shortest way possible.

To Them That Have is Debreuil's third feature film and <u>it is his best movie yet</u>[0]. Critics, including myself, admired his early promise but <u>we wondered</u>[1] if he would produce a film worthy of that promise, and now <u>he has produced a film worthy of that promise</u>[2].

The film starts and <u>it finishes</u>[3] in 19th century France, but the story spans four continents and <u>spans three centuries</u>[4], and <u>the story follows the lives of three families</u>[5]. The dialogue is fast and <u>it is witty</u>[6]. You would expect the photography to be stunning in a Debrueil film, and <u>it is stunning</u>[7].

Should you go and see this film? Yes, <u>you must go and see this film</u>[8].

Star rating: ★★★★★

0 his best movie yet   5 ....
1 ....   6 ....
2 ....   7 ....
3 ....   8 ....
4 ....

C After the film

A group of students read the review and went to see the film. Afterwards, they talked about it in a café. Look at their conversation and cross out ten unnecessary words or phrases. The first is done for you.

ZAC   I thought it was great but ~~I thought it was~~ too long. The main actress was beautiful and was very talented.

ALFIE   Yes, but I didn't like the soundtrack or I didn't like the fact that it was in black and white.

BORIS   Well, I thought the film would annoy me, but it didn't annoy me.

ALFIE   Anyway, shall we have another drink?

BORIS   Well, I wasn't planning to have another drink, but OK, I will have another drink.

ZAC   I can't have another drink, I'm afraid. I've got to go.

ALFIE   Do you really have to go?

ZAC   Well, I should go. I'm staying at my brother's house tonight and he goes to bed early, so he probably expects me to go to bed early as well.

5 In a defining relative clause with **be**, we can leave out **who, which** or **that + be**. **Who, which** or **that** can refer to the subject, the object or the indirect object.

SUBJECT
The man who is in the corner waved at me.
→ The man in the corner waved at me.

OBJECT
I watched the man who was in the corner.
→ I watched the man in the corner.

INDIRECT OBJECT
I gave a cake to the man who was in the corner.
→ I gave a cake to the man in the corner.

6 When the form of **be** is part of a continuous verb, we can leave out **who, which** or **that + be**:

I like the woman who is talking to Peter.
→ I like the woman talking to Peter.

7 When the form of **be** is part of a passive form, we can leave out **who, which** or **that + be**:

I spoke to the man who is known as Lucky Leslie.
→ I spoke to the man known as Lucky Leslie.

(For more information on defining relative clauses, see p. 110.)

> We often use **one** instead of repeating a noun:
> *Which car do you mean? ~ The car which is in front of mine.*
> → *The car in front of mine.*
> → *The **one** in front of mine.*
>
> TIP

Grammar in action

8 In spoken English we often leave words out of defining relative clauses, and use *-ing* forms or past participles. We are still able to explain which person or thing we are talking about, but it is often more normal to leave words out when the meaning is clear:

Can you see that man? ~ Which man? ~ The one standing at the top of the ladder over there.

D At the wedding

Tom and Cara are at Tom's cousin's wedding. Tom has not seen a lot of his family for a long time, and it is the first time that Cara has met some of them. Complete their conversation, choosing the correct form of the verb in brackets.

TOM   My uncle Jack is the man _____talking_____ [0] (talk) to the bride.

CARA   Which man? There are three men _____ [1] (stand) with the bride.

TOM   Yes, sorry. He's the tall one _____ [2] (move) his hands a lot.

CARA   Is he the uncle _____ [3] (marry) to the former model?

TOM   Yes, that's right, Auntie Rita. She's the one _____ [4] (mention) in *Vogue* the other day.

CARA   Oh yes, I remember. They said she was the model _____ [5] (photograph) the most in the early 1980s.

TOM   Yes. You see the two women _____ [6] (sit) at the table on the left? Well, Rita is the lady _____ [7] (wear) the orange hat. The person _____ [8] (talk) to her is her daughter, my cousin Jo.

CARA   OK. I'll never remember all this.

E   People in a photo

Complete the sentences about who is who using *next to*, *between*, *behind* and *in front of*.

0   Molly is <u>the woman between</u> Jenny and Lara.

1   Nick is .... Jenny.

2   Jenny is .... Molly.

3   Lara is .... Peter.

4   Peter is .... Jessica.

5   Molly is .... Lara and Jenny.

Now answer the questions in the shortest way possible.

6   Who's the man behind Jenny? ....

....

7   Where's Jessica? ....

....

8   What's the name of the woman in front of Nick?

....

F   Unnecessary words

Rewrite these sentences, omitting any unnecessary words.

0   I just read a book that is called *How To Win Friends And Influence People*.

<u>I just read a book called How To Win Friends And Influence People.</u>

1   Pelé is the footballer who is often described as the greatest footballer of all time.

....

2   James Earl Jones is an actor who is best known as the voice of Darth Vader in the *Star Wars* films.

....

3   I passed the message to the policeman who was waiting outside the door.

....

4   The finest bananas in the world are the ones that are grown in Madagascar.

....

5   Computers which are built in China are cheaper than British ones.

....

6   Apples which are bought from a greengrocer's usually taste better than supermarket apples.

....

OVER TO YOU   Now go to page 125.

Over to you

01 Present simple and present continuous

Write an introductory letter to a new penfriend to tell him/her about yourself and your family, where you live and what you do. Use the **present simple**.

Imagine that you are at the beach or in the park, speaking to a friend on your phone. Your friend wants to know what you can see. Describe what the people around you are doing, using the **present continuous**.

Think of three or four activities that you might have arranged to do with your friends. Then imagine that some other friends ask you to to do something with them at the same time as those activities. Explain to them that you can't go with them because you are doing something else, using the **present simple** and the **present continuous**.

02 Talking about the past

Say or write down three things that you have done in your life that you are proud of and your age when it happened, using the **past simple**, for example, 'When I was 14, I won a poetry competition.'

Can you remember what was happening and what you and your friends or family were doing when you heard about the attack on the Twin Towers in New York on 11 September 2001? Say or write three things, using the **past continuous**, and starting with 'When I heard about the attack, I was …'

Say or write three things that you did in the past, but that you don't do any more, using **used to**.

03 Present perfect

Say or write down three things that you have done in your life and that you think none of your friends have done, using the **present perfect**.

Then think about your best friend and say or write down three things that you think he/she has never done, using the **present perfect**.

Say or write down three things about yourself that have never changed, using **always** and the **present perfect**.

Say or write down three things that you have been doing, and say how long you have been doing them using **for** or **since** and the **present perfect continuous**.

04 Past simple and present perfect; past perfect

Imagine that you are looking after a friend's dog for a few days. One day you go shopping and leave the dog at home alone. When you come back, you find the dog has ruined your home! Describe to your friend what happened while you were out of the house, using the **past perfect** and starting with 'When I got back home, …'

Working with a friend, ask and answer questions about your daily routines, comparing things you have done today with things you did yesterday. Use the **present perfect** when you ask about today, and the **past simple** when you ask about yesterday, for example, 'Have you spoken to Simon today? Did you speak to Simon yesterday?'

05 The future

Imagine that you have booked your dream holiday. Describe to a friend what you are going to do, where you are going to stay and how you are going to get there using **going to**.

How do you predict the world will change in the next fifty years? Write down three things that you think will happen in the future, using **will** and starting with 'In the next fifty years, …'

How can you help your parents around the home? Write down three suggestions or offers of help, using **will** and **shall**.

▶

06 Ability, permission, and requests

Say or write three things that you couldn't do when you were younger but that you can now do, using **couldn't** and **can** and starting with 'When I was younger, …'.

Say or write three things that you will be able to do when you've finished your studies, using **will be able to** and starting with 'When I finish my studies, …'.

Write a dialogue between two people having lunch together. Use **would** and **please** as much as possible.

07 Possibility and probability; perfect modals

Imagine that you have arranged to meet a friend, but he is late. Suggest three things that might have happened to him/her, using **may**, **might**, and **could**.

Think about what you might do after you have finished your studies at school, and write three of them, using **may**, **might**, and **could**, and starting with 'After I've finished my studies at school, …'.

How do you think the ancient Egyptians built the pyramids? Suggest some things that they must have done, and some things they can't have done, and the reasons why, using **must have** and **can't have + past participle**.

08 Duty and obligation

Imagine that your friend has returned home to find that someone has burgled his/her house. He/she has called you to ask what he/she should do. Give some suggestions, using **should**, **shouldn't** or **ought to**.

Think of three interesting jobs and describe the duties associated with each one, using **have to**.

09 Infinitives and *-ing* forms (1)

Imagine you went on a sightseeing trip of London yesterday. Describe which parts of the day you enjoyed and which parts you didn't enjoy, using **like** or **enjoy**, **didn't like** or **didn't enjoy** + *-ing* **form**.

What kind of parent will you be? Describe how you will treat your children, using verbs like **help**, **encourage**, **want**, **love**, **persuade**, **prefer**, **teach** + **object** + **infinitive**.

10 Infinitives and *-ing* forms (2)

Imagine that next week you have to take part in the following activities: swimming, parachuting, writing poetry, reading, skiing. Describe how you feel about doing each of these activities or how good you are at them, using an **adjective** + **preposition** + *-ing* **form.**

11 The passive

Use the internet to research the following subjects, then write a sentence or two about each, using the **passive**, giving details such as who invented/wrote/designed/built it and when: *The Importance Of Being Ernest*; the Sydney Opera House; the telephone; the Eiffel Tower; *The Deer Hunter*; the ceiling of the Sistine Chapel; *The Lord Of The Rings*

Imagine you were a member of the town council. What changes would you make to your town? Say or write three sentences using **have** + **object** + **past participle**.

12 Phrasal and prepositional verbs

Write three phrasal or prepositional verbs with the preposition **up**, three with the preposition **in**, and three with the preposition **on**. Then write a sentence for each, to indicate that you understand its meaning.

13 Indirect speech (1)

Imagine that you overheard a conversation in which two men, Pat and Ted, were planning a bank robbery. Report what you heard to the police, using **indirect speech**. Include as many details as you can, including any questions that you heard the two men ask each other.

14 Indirect speech (2)

Imagine you have given a friend directions from the train station to your house. Report the instructions you gave to your friend. Use indirect speech and verbs like **tell**, **remind**, and **warn**.

15 Conditional sentences

Think of three events in your future that you are worried about, for example exams or a driving test, and explain why you are worried about them by imagining what will happen if they go badly. Use **first conditionals**.

Think about three things that you would like to change about yourself or your life. Then explain why you would like these things to change by describing what you would do if things were different. Use the **second conditional**.

16 Nouns

Describe where you keep things at home, using as many **noun + noun** structures as you can.

17 Possessives

Think about your friends and relatives, list their hobbies and any gadgets they might have, and compare them with your own. Use as many different **possessive adjectives** and **possessive pronouns** as you can. For example, 'My dad's hobby is cycling. My hobby is running.', 'My brother and I both have iPods. His is more expensive than mine.', etc.

18 Demonstratives

Imagine you and your friends are shopping for clothes. Write a dialogue of the sort of things you would say to each other when you are comparing items in a shop. Explain which clothes you like, which clothes you don't like, and use as many different **demonstratives** (**this**, **that**, **these** and **those**) as you can.

19 Quantifiers

List the food that you have in your fridge, and write what food you will need to buy when you go shopping. Use as many of the following quantifiers as possible: **some**, **any**, **no**, **much**, **many**, **a few**, **a little**, **a lot of**. Start with 'In my fridge, I have …'

Imagine you are a company director and you are interviewing a job applicant. First, describe the people in your company using **everyone**, **everybody** and **no one**. Then describe the ideal candidate for the job, using sentences with **somebody**, **someone** and **anybody** and starting with 'I'm looking for …' or 'I'm not looking for …'.

20 Comparative and superlative forms

Guinness World Records is a book which lists the greatest human achievements and the extremes of the natural world. Can you think of any people, places or things that are world record holders? Name them and explain why they should be in *Guinness World Records*, comparing them with similar people, places or things, using **superlatives** and **comparatives**. For example, 'The Nile is the longest river in the world. It is longer than the Thames.'

How is your life easier or harder than your parents' or your grandparents'? Compare your life with theirs using **comparatives** and **comparative + than** structures.

21 *(Not) as … as, enough, too*

Imagine that you went to a party recently, but it wasn't as good as you expected it to be. Write some sentences to explain what the problems were, using **not as … as**, **enough** and **too**.

Imagine that you have a little brother who is only 14. He wants to go on holiday to the US with his friends. What would your parents say to him? Write some sentences using **not … enough** and **too**.

22 Adverbs

Think of your favourite recipe and write instructions, using as many **adverbs** as you can.

23 Connecting adverbs

Imagine you and your friends are on a camping trip. You need to find a good place to set up your camp, put up your tents, and cook some food. Write a dialogue in which you and your friends discuss the trip and how to do these things, using as many **connecting adverbs** (**so**, **too**, **either**, **neither**, **first**, **next**, **then**, **actually**, **fortunately**, **only**, **even**, etc.) as you can.

24 Prepositions (1)

Summarize the plot of a film that you have seen recently, explaining the attitudes of the characters and their feelings towards each other and the things in the story, using as many **prepositions** and **prepositional phrases** as you can.

25 Prepositions (2)

Describe the room you are sitting in, using as many **prepositions** and **prepositional phrases** as you can.

Think of someone you know who has changed his or her lifestyle. Describe the changes he or she has made and explain why, using as many of the **prepositional phrases** on p. 100 as you can.

26 Linking words

Imagine you are writing an advertisement for an exciting new gadget that has two uses. Name it and write a few sentences to explain why you need it and what it does, using linking words such as **because**, **for**, **both … and**, **either … or**, **in order to**, and **so that**. Start with 'The … is an amazing gadget: …'.

27 Linking sentences

We are damaging the environment and our planet is in danger. Write some sentences using **if … not**, **unless**, **in case**, **furthermore**, **moreover**, **what's more,** etc. to explain the danger, suggest some changes we should make and describe what will happen if we don't make those changes.

Do you believe in aliens? Do you believe that life exists on other planets? Write a few sentences explaining the arguments for and against, using **but**, **though**, **however**, and **on the other hand**.

28 Relative clauses

Write sentences using **relative clauses** to explain briefly who each of these people are/were and why they are famous: William Shakespeare, J.K. Rowling, Bill Gates, Charles Babbage, George Lucas. Start with ' … is the man/woman who …'. Then think of a few more famous people and write sentences for them, too.

Imagine you are writing an article for a travel guide. Describe your favourite city, using as many **relative clauses** as you can.

29 Expressions of time, place, and reason

Write a dialogue in which you and your childhood best friend remember some things that you did together when you were younger. Use as many of the **time expressions** on p. 114 as possible.

30 Leaving out words

Say or write three things that were true when you were younger but which are now different, leaving out any unnecessary repetition of words. For example: 'When I was younger, I couldn't swim but now I can.', 'When I was younger nobody had computers, but now everyone does.'

Form tables

A Plural nouns

	SINGULAR	PLURAL
+ -s		
With most nouns, we add **-s** to make them plural:	shop	shop**s**
	tyre	tyre**s**
	kilo	kilo**s**
+ -es		
With nouns that end with **-s, -ss, -sh, -ch** and **-x** we add **-es**:	bus	bus**es**
	dress	dress**es**
	wish	wish**es**
	beach	beach**es**
	box	box**es**
+ -es		
With some nouns that end with **-o**, we add **-es**:	tomato	tomato**es**
	potato	potato**es**
-f/-fe ⟶ -ves		
We change **-f/-fe** to **-ves** in the plural:	thief	thie**ves**
	shelf	shel**ves**
	leaf	lea**ves**
	life	li**ves**
-y ⟶ -ies		
With nouns that end with a consonant* + **-y**, we change the **-y** to **-ies**:	story	stor**ies**
	copy	cop**ies**
	lorry	lorr**ies**
Irregular nouns		
	tooth	teeth
	child	children
	woman	women

B   Uncountable nouns

These are some common uncountable nouns:	**ice, water, rain, snow, heat, noise, cotton, glass, petrol, money, luggage, information, work, homework, advice, news, meat, milk, butter, bread, marmalade, food, tea, coffee, sugar, toast, cheese**
Uncountable nouns do not have a plural form:	**petrol** (NOT **petrols**) **bread** (NOT **breads**)
We cannot use **a/an** with an uncountable noun, but we can use **some/any, the, much** (NOT **many**), **such**, and **my/your/his** etc.:	**a**: *I always have an egg, then **toast** and **marmalade** for breakfast.* **some**: *I'd like **some tea** please.* **the**: *Look at **the snow** outside.* **much**: *How **much luggage** have you got?* **such**: *We've had **such wonderful news**.*
Some nouns can be countable or uncountable:	*I heard **a noise** from downstairs.* (countable) *I can't sleep. The neighbours are making **so much noise**.* (uncountable)

* Consonants
b c d f g h j k
l m n p q r s t
v w x y z

Vowels
a e i o u

Syllables
|hit| = 1 syllable
|vi|sit| = 2 syllables
|re|mem|ber| = 3 syllables

C   Present simple

	I/YOU/WE/THEY	HE/SHE/IT
+ -s		
After **he/she/it**, we add **-s** to most Present simple verbs:	say	say**s**
	make	make**s**
	advise	advise**s**
+ -es		
We add **-es** to verbs that end with **-ss**, **-sh**, **-ch**, **-o** or **-x** (e.g. finish, go):	pass	pass**es**
	finish	finish**es**
	wish	wish**es**
	catch	catch**es**
	go	go**es**
	do	do**es**
-y → -ies		
We change **-y** to **-ies** with verbs that end with a consonant* + **-y**:	fly	fl**ies**
	carry	carr**ies**
	study	stud**ies**

D   *-ing* forms

	INFINITIVE	-ING FORM
+-ing		
With most verbs we add **-ing**:	go	go**ing**
	ask	ask**ing**
-e + -ing		
With verbs that end with a consonant* + **-e**, we delete the **-e** and add **-ing**:	take	tak**ing**
	hope	hop**ing**
	live	liv**ing**
	queue	queu**ing**
-ie → -ying		
With verbs that end with **-ie**, we change **-ie** to **-ying**:	lie	l**ying**
	die	d**ying**
-t → -tting		
With verbs that end with one vowel* + one consonant (e.g. *run*, *swim*, *jog*), we double the consonant:	get	get**ting**
	run	run**ning**
	swim	swim**ming**
	jog	jog**ging**
+ -ing		
But note that we do not double the consonant, 1) when it is **y** or **w** (e.g. *stay*) 2) when the last syllable* is not stressed (e.g. *VISit*, *LISTen*, *WONder*):	stay	stay**ing**
	buy	buy**ing**
	borrow	borrow**ing**
	draw	draw**ing**
	visit	visit**ing**
	listen	listen**ing**
But not also that we double the **l** at the end of the verbs, when the last syllable is not stressed (e.g. *TRAvel*):	wonder	wonder**ing**
	travel	trave**lling**

E   Regular verbs: Past simple and past participle

	INFINITIVE	PAST SIMPLE	PAST PARTICIPLE
+ -ed			
With most verbs, we add -**ed**:	happen	happen**ed**	happen**ed**
+ -d			
With verbs ending with -**e**, we add -**d**:	live	live**d**	live**d**
-y ⟶ -ied			
With verbs that end with one consonant* + -**y**, we change the -**y** to -**ied**:	try	tr**ied**	tr**ied**
	study	stud**ied**	stud**ied**
-p ⟶ -pped			
With verbs that end with one vowel* + one consonant (e.g. *stop*), we double the consonant:	stop	sto**pped**	sto**pped**
	grab	gra**bbed**	gra**bbed**
+ -ed			
But note that we do not double the consonant,	enjoy	enjoy**ed**	enjoy**ed**
1) when it is **y** or **w** (e.g. *play*)	allow	allow**ed**	allow**ed**
2) when the last syllable* is not stressed (e.g. *LISten, Happen, Open*):	discover	discover**ed**	discover**ed**
	listen	listen**ed**	listen**ed**
Note that in British English **l** is usually doubled, even if the syllable is unstressed (e.g. *TRAvel*):	cancel	cance**lled**	cance**lled**
	travel	trave**lled**	trave**lled**

F   Irregular verbs: Past simple and past participle

INFINITIVE	PAST SIMPLE	PAST PARTICIPLE
be	was/were	been
beat	beat	beaten
become	became	become
begin	began	begun
break	broke	broken
bring	brought	brought
build	built	built
burn	burnt	burnt
buy	bought	bought
catch	caught	caught
choose	chose	chosen
come	came	come
cost	cost	cost
cut	cut	cut
do	did	done
draw	drew	drawn
drink	drank	drunk
drive	drove	driven
eat	ate	eaten
fall	fell	fallen
feel	felt	felt
find	found	found
fly	flew	flown
forget	forgot	forgotten
forbid	forbade	forbidden
get	got	got
give	gave	given
go	went	gone/been
grow	grew	grown
have	had	had
hear	heard	heard
hide	hid	hidden
hit	hit	hit
hold	held	held
hurt	hurt	hurt
keep	kept	kept
know	knew	known

INFINITIVE	PAST SIMPLE	PAST PARTICIPLE
learn	learnt/learned	learnt/learned
leave	left	left
lend	lent	lent
let	let	let
lose	lost	lost
make	made	made
meet	met	met
pay	paid	paid
put	put	put
read	read	read
ring	rang	rung
run	ran	run
say	said	said
see	saw	seen
sell	sold	sold
send	sent	sent
show	showed	shown/showed
shut	shut	shut
sing	sang	sung
sit	sat	sat
sleep	slept	slept
speak	spoke	spoken
spend	spent	spent
stand	stood	stood
steal	stole	stolen
sweep	swept	swept
swim	swam	swum
take	took	taken
teach	taught	taught
tell	told	told
think	thought	thought
throw	threw	thrown
understand	understood	understood
wake	woke	woken
wear	wore	worn
win	won	won
write	wrote	written

G   Comparative and superlative adjectives

	ADJECTIVE	COMPARATIVE	SUPERLATIVE
+ -er/-est			
We add **-er/-est** to short adjectives (one-syllable* adjectives):	cheap near long	cheap**er** near**er** long**er**	the cheap**est** the near**est** the long**est**
+ -r/-st			
We add **-r/-st** to adjectives that end with **-e**:	late	late**r**	the late**st**
+ -g → -gger			
With short adjectives that end with one vowel* and one consonant* (e.g. *big*), we double the consonant:	big hot wet	bi**gger** ho**tter** we**tter**	the bi**ggest** the ho**ttest** the we**ttest**
-w + -er / -est			
We don't double **-w**:	low	low**er**	low**est**
more / most			
We use **more / the most** before adjectives of two or more syllables*:	expensive beautiful polluted	**more** expensive **more** beautiful **more** polluted	**the most** expensive **the most** beautiful **the most** polluted
-y → -ier / -iest			
But note that with adjectives ending with **-y** (e.g. *happy*), we change **-y** to **-ier / -iest:**	happ**y** luck**y** eas**y** **dirty**	happ**ier** luck**ier** eas**ier** **dirtier**	the happ**iest** the luck**iest** the eas**iest** the dirt**iest**
Irregular adjectives:			
	good bad far little	better worse further less	the best the worst the farthest the least
fewer and less			
Note that we use **fewer** with plural nouns, and **less** with uncountable nouns (e.g. *money*):	There are **fewer** shops in the centre of town than there used to be. John earns **less** money than Mary.		

Verb tables

A   Verb tenses

	POSITIVE	NEGATIVE	QUESTIONS
Present simple			
	I **know** the answer Jane **walks** to school.	I **don't cook** very well. She **doesn't like** him.	Do you **like** Indian food? Does John **drive** to work?
Present continuous			
	I'm **writing** a letter. He's **reading** a book. They're **playing** football.	I'm **not sleeping**. It **isn't working**. We **aren't using** it at the moment.	Am I **winning**? Is she **waiting** for you? What **are** you **cooking**?
Past simple			
	I **cooked** the dinner last night	They **didn't have** a holiday last year.	Did you **see** John yesterday?
Past continuous			
	She **was watching** the TV. We **were talking** to the doctor.	The fridge **wasn't working**. They **weren't enjoying** the film.	Was it **raining**? Where **were** you **staying**.
Present perfect			
	I've **lost** my car keys. He's **found** a new job.	We **haven't paid** the bill. It **hasn't rained** for weeks.	Have you **heard** the news. Has the train **arrived** yet?
Present perfect continuous			
	We've **been staying** with some friends. He's **been saving** his money for a holiday.	You **haven't been doing** well at school. He **hasn't been running**.	Have you **been waiting** long? What **have** you **been doing**?
Past perfect			
	I **had posted** the letter.	He **hadn't arrived**.	Had it **finished**?

B   Verb structures

MODAL + INFINITIVE		
She	**can**	swim.
He	**could**	be (right).
Jane	**may**	be (at home).
It	**might**	come (tomorrow).
I	**must**	finish (this today).
You	**needn't**	go (to the shops).
I	**shall**	arrive (at six o'clock).
You	**should**	ask (her).
Mark	**will**	be (happy).
Tom	**would**	like (to come).

VERB + -ING FORM		
James	**enjoys**	travelling.
They've	**finished**	repairing (the car).
He	**keeps**	asking (questions).
She's	**stopped**	smoking.

VERB + TO + INFINITIVE		
I	**decided**	to go (to America).
She	**hopes**	to get (a job soon).
We	**ought**	to tell (the police).
I	**promise**	to write (to you).
He	**refused**	to talk (to me).
She	**used**	to smoke.
Jane	**wants**	to be (a doctor).

Answer key

01 Present simple and present continuous

A
1 includes
2 rescue
3 pump
4 don't … work
5 phones
6 sends
7 doesn't work
8 do
9 have
10 equals

B
1 're looking
2 are … behaving
3 being
4 's … doing
5 's building
6 is … helping
7 's sitting
8 's trying
9 are … talking
10 's asking
11 'm drawing
12 'm concentrating

C
1 eat
2 'm trying
3 looks
4 means
5 doesn't eat
6 's suffering
7 thinks
8 seems
9 don't kill
10 agree
11 believes
12 hope

WORD FOCUS   A strict   B to exploit

D
1 does … leave
2 leaves
3 don't arrive
4 take
5 lasts
6 do … begin
7 have
8 doesn't leave
9 gets
10 's
11 doesn't start

E
1 're meeting
2 does … begin
3 'm taking
4 doesn't leave
5 Are … doing
6 are going
7 are … getting
8 're leaving
9 'm not doing

F
1 I'm afraid we can't meet on Tuesday afternoon because I'm playing tennis with Peter.
2 I'm sorry I can't see you on Thursday afternoon because I'm helping Sam move into his new flat.
3 Friday is no good. I'm having lunch with the boss. Anyway, I'm seeing you on Saturday.
4 Sorry, I'm going shopping with my mum on Saturday morning. Are you doing anything in the evening?

02 Talking about the past

A
1 was spending
2 set
3 reached
4 made
5 didn't start
6 arrived
7 weren't planning
8 was shining
9 was walking
10 decided
11 were having
12 was playing
13 stopped
14 announced
15 added
16 were you
17 happened
18 was lying
19 had
20 was watching
21 wasn't enjoying
22 didn't think
23 interrupted
24 were you doing
25 heard
26 was walking
27 got
28 sent
29 was wearing
30 didn't believe
31 called
32 told

B
1 didn't have
2 spent
3 had
4 started
5 had
6 were working
7 was painting
8 was putting
9 fell
10 wasn't being
11 worked
12 didn't finish
13 did you do
14 Did you see
15 mentioned
16 did you go

C
1 used to be
2 didn't use to go
3 didn't use to have
4 used to live
5 used to go
6 didn't use to drink

D
1 was
2 ✓
3 was raining
4 used to keep
5 ✓
6 didn't understand

E
1 used to play
2 wasn't playing
3 used to watch
4 was watching
5 noticed
6 was wearing
7 didn't use to wear / didn't wear
8 thought
9 won
10 decided
11 knew
12 happened
13 arrived
14 used to get / got
15 had
16 looked
17 was holding
18 arranged
19 didn't have
20 started
21 became
22 stopped
23 was expecting
24 used to love / loved
25 were playing

03 Present perfect

A
1 all my life
2 ever
3 just
4 ever
5 never
6 already
7 several times
8 yet

B
1 've had
2 've been
3 've had
4 have found
5 still hasn't graduated
6 hasn't been
7 has often worked
8 've managed
9 has sent
10 've visited
11 've spent
12 've written
13 has already sold
14 has just paid
15 has just asked

C
1 Ruth has just phoned
2 she still hasn't left
3 she's done
4 have you bought
5 I haven't bought anything yet
6 I've just ordered
7 I've already asked
8 She's got
9 she's promised
10 have you found
11 I've asked
12 still haven't phoned back
13 I've persuaded
14 I've just checked

D
1 've been waiting
2 have you been standing
3 Has it been raining
4 've been coming
5 've been writing
6 've been trying

E
1 have you been doing
2 've been playing
3 've been building
4 've been feeding
5 've been worrying

F
1 has promised
2 Have you all been getting on
3 have been making
4 've made
5 have you managed
6 've been working
7 haven't solved
8 've been moving
9 has wiped
10 've been expecting
11 has agreed

04 Past simple and present perfect; past perfect

A
1 came
2 've met
3 met
4 stayed
5 hasn't slept
6 got
7 've been
8 've really enjoyed
9 read
10 set off
11 did
12 've eaten
13 recommended
14 went
15 have you visited
16 was
17 decided
18 've never climbed

B
1 has changed
2 lived
3 haven't visited
4 has become
5 produced / used to produce
6 have closed
7 got
8 didn't agree
9 liked
10 have brought

WORD FOCUS got rid of

C
1 'd created
2 had seen
3 'd told
4 'd been
5 'd never caused
6 had … stolen
7 had made
8 had put
9 had fallen
10 had noticed
11 hadn't taken
12 had apologized

D
1 had been
2 hadn't finished
3 had sent
4 had received
5 had … written
6 hadn't arrived
7 had phoned
8 had agreed
9 had left

05 The future

A
1 1
2 1
3 3
4 4
5 1
6 2

B
1 'm going to send
2 'm not going to write
3 'm going to do
4 's going to help
5 are going to watch
6 'm not going to revise
7 'm going to revise
8 'm going to prepare
9 'm going to show

C
1 are … going to attract
2 is going to clean
3 is going to improve
4 is going to renovate
5 are not going to install
6 is going to disappoint
7 are going to upgrade
8 is going to employ
9 Are … going to get
10 are not going to get

D
1 will
2 won't
3 will
4 will
5 won't
6 will
7 won't
8 will
9 will
10 will
11 won't
12 will
13 will
14 won't
15 will

E
1	Will	5	will / shall	9	won't
2	shall	6	won't / shan't	10	Shall
3	Shall	7	will / shall		
4	will	8	will / shall		

WORD FOCUS   put up with

F
1 'll call; warning
2 'll help; offer
3 'll go; spontaneous decision
4 're going to drive; decision made in advance
5 'll buy; promise

06 Ability, permission, and requests

A
1	couldn't	7	couldn't	13	can
2	could	8	can	14	can
3	can	9	can't	15	can
4	could	10	could	16	can't
5	can	11	can	17	couldn't
6	could	12	could	18	can't

WORD FOCUS   A previously   B enormous
C benefits

B
1	can't	4	be able	7	were able
2	couldn't	5	could	8	can
3	can't	6	managed	9	will be able

C
1 Can you invite Mr Jones for an interview, please?
2 Could you take a message, please?
3 Would you ask Jim to email me, please?
4 Would you collect the report from reception, please?

D
1	could organize	8	weren't allowed
2	Could you	9	be able
3	managed to book	10	you help
4	couldn't	11	we can
5	I'll be able	12	managed to
6	could	13	you'll be able to help
7	can		

E
1	May	6	managed to
2	can't	7	couldn't
3	Can	8	want
4	Could	9	can
5	can	10	be able to

07 Possibility and probability; perfect modals

A
1	must cost	3	must think	5	must have
2	can't love	4	can't mean	6	can't be

B
1	may want	3	may not come	5	may not get
2	may not have	4	may decide	6	may be

C
1 may / might go
2 can't be
3 may not / might not renew
4 may / might take
5 must have
6 may / might find
7 may not / might not want
8 can't be

WORD FOCUS   a grant

D
1	can't have been	6	may have been
2	may have died	7	can't have killed
3	can't have drowned	8	must have seen
4	must have died	9	can't have had
5	must have had	10	must have been

E
1	must have learned/learnt	5	might have been
2	might have posed	6	must have met
3	might have had	7	can't have imagined
4	can't have been	8	might have invented

08 Duty and obligation

A
1	should … dress	5	should … behave
2	shouldn't wear / choose	6	shouldn't look
3	should choose / wear	7	should show
4	should wash		

B
1	should / have to	5	have to	9	should
2	shouldn't	6	ought to	10	shouldn't
3	shouldn't	7	don't have to	11	have to
4	ought not to	8	should		

C
1	should / have to	4	have to	7	should
2	do I have to	5	should	8	shouldn't
3	don't have to	6	have to	9	should

D
1	mustn't	5	must	9	don't have to
2	don't have to	6	must	10	mustn't
3	must	7	mustn't		
4	mustn't	8	mustn't		

WORD FOCUS   B

E
1	do … need to	5	need	9	needs to
2	need to	6	don't need to	10	don't need to
3	don't need	7	need to		
4	needs	8	needs to		

F
1	don't have to	5	must	9	should
2	should	6	must	10	ought to
3	must	7	don't have to		
4	mustn't	8	must		

09 Infinitives and -ing forms (1)

A
1	cycling	5	sharing	9	to give
2	walking	6	to show	10	to mention
3	escaping	7	to spend		
4	doing	8	to beat		

B
1	to spend	6	to start	11	to decide
2	to look	7	to work	12	working
3	to go	8	to encourage	13	organizing
4	to find	9	to organize	14	meeting
5	to study	10	taking	15	earning

WORD FOCUS A abroad B accepted

C
1	plan to take	6	hope to make
2	need to think	7	keep on raising
3	refuse to pay	8	threaten to go
4	go shopping	9	decide to change
5	manage to put		

D
1 My brother taught me to play the guitar.
2 My mother expected me to go to university.
3 My father wanted me to study engineering.
4 When I first met my manager, he persuaded me to give him a chance.
5 My manager helped me to get a record deal.
6 The famous musicians, 'The Rolling Faces', invited me to join their tour.

E
1	let her choose	6	make her go
2	permitted her to study	7	remind you to aim
3	expected her to do	8	let me help
4	deserves to be	9	warn you to work
5	encourage her to apply		

F
1 They encouraged him to take
2 they didn't want anyone to steal
3 they reminded Sean to take
4 he failed to take
5 he expected it to be
6 His friends helped him look
7 They decided to call
8 they persuaded Sean to tell
9 they had warned him not to forget
10 they wouldn't let Sean take

10 Infinitives and -ing forms (2)

A
1	to see	4	to go
2	thinking	5	to show
3	to think	6	showing

B
1 stopped trying
2 like to see
3 liked playing / liked to play
4 remember to contact
5 prefer to watch
6 remember going
7 tried not to cry
8 stopped supporting
9 stopped growing
10 hated being / hated to be
11 started liking / started to like
12 forget to meet

C
1	to tell	7	modelling
2	going / to go	8	to talk
3	to study	9	being / to be
4	to relax	10	to get
5	doing / to do		
6	to work		

D
1 is hopeless at working in a team
2 are afraid of using / afraid to use a computer
3 are brilliant at using a computer
4 is very keen on writing reports
5 is not interested in talking to customers
6 is excited about talking to customers
7 is terrible at answering the telephone
8 are incapable of answering the telephone

E
1	swimming	4	being	7	to bring
2	windsurfing	5	seeing	8	to collect
3	sunbathing	6	finding	9	remembering

WORD FOCUS A race out B finding out

11 The passive

A
1 Grapes are grown in many countries. About half are eaten as fruit and half are made into wine.
2 Nowadays, most fruit is washed before it is sold to the public.
3 At sea, fish are frozen as soon as they are caught.
4 Some fish are kept in fish farms. They are fed with food that is produced in a factory.
5 Oranges are often picked when they are green because they are transported thousands of miles.
6 Flour is made from cereal grains such as wheat and rye. It is used to make bread and cakes.

B
1 Who was the Mona Lisa painted by? It was painted by Leonardo da Vinci, an Italian artist.
2 Who was penicillin discovered by? It was discovered by Alexander Fleming, a Scottish scientist.
3 Who was the television invented by? It was invented by John Logie Baird, a Scottish scientist.
4 Who were the Harry Potter books written by? They were written by J. K. Rowling, a British author.
5 Who was the 100m sprint at the Beijing Olympics won by? It was won by Usain Bolt, a Jamaican athlete.
6 Who were the pyramids built by? They were built by the ancient Egyptians.

C
1 A few minutes later, a fire was found in the school kitchen.
2 The fire started because a cooker had been left on.
3 The fire brigade was notified a few minutes ago.
4 The school has been evacuated.
5 All the students have been counted.
6 The school is being checked to make sure no one is still inside.
7 The students are being allowed to go home early.

D
1 has all her fan mail answered
2 had her hair coloured
3 is going to have her photo taken
4 had a special dress made
5 has had her teeth whitened
6 is having her flat decorated

E
1 have been installed
2 will be needed / are needed
3 be spent
4 was given
5 be decided
6 is expected
7 were promised
8 be trusted
9 had … painted
10 have done
11 have … checked
12 be replaced
13 were told
14 be left
15 are taken

12 Phrasal and prepositional verbs

A
1 it on
2 him up
3 it out / it away
4 them off
5 it down
6 them in
7 it up
8 them up
9 you back
10 me off

B
1 check in
2 took off
3 fill it in
4 gave up
5 sorted out
6 turn it off
7 hang on
8 look up
9 dress up
10 go on
11 tire me out
12 get up

C
1 put
2 away
3 fall
4 out
5 shut
6 up
7 turn
8 on
9 go
10 out
11 give
12 up
13 carry
14 on

D
1 I'm glad you're getting over your infection.
2 Is Sally looking after you?
3 You won't feel like visitors at the moment.
4 But call on us when you come to London.
5 We're looking forward to seeing you.

E
1 stands for
2 look after
3 looking for
4 consist of
5 deal with
6 pay for
7 find out
8 think about

F
1 get on with
2 put up with
3 feels like it
4 puts them off
5 get away with it
6 tell him off
7 broken down
8 find out
9 run out of
10 asked for
11 filling in
12 put it away
13 look for
14 carry on
15 applied for
WORD FOCUS A puts them off B get away with it

13 Indirect speech (1)

A
1 (that) she was going to France
2 (that) his mother had given him £50
3 (that) they had moved into their new house
4 (that) she couldn't finish her essay
5 (that) he would remind John about our meeting
6 (that) the parcels had arrived safely

B
1 the month before / the previous month
2 the week before
3 had cleared
4 a couple of weeks before/earlier
5 hadn't arrived
6 were coming
7 the following month / the month after

C
1 told
2 had come
3 said
4 had decided
5 asked
6 if/whether he lived
7 told
8 had lived
9 asked
10 where I lived
11 said/replied
12 had
13 told
14 was going
15 asked
16 if/whether I wanted
17 said/replied
18 couldn't
19 were coming

D
1 her (that) I had enjoyed
2 (that) I had always preferred
3 (me) if/whether I had
4 (that) I didn't, but I spoke
5 visited
6 what I did
7 her (that) I was
8 (that) I worked
9 if/whether I had done
10 (that) everybody had to do
11 could start
12 wasn't
13 I would
14 wasn't
15 if/whether there were
16 was looking for
17 she would speak to him
18 said

14 Indirect speech (2)

A
1	her	11	had	21	pointed out
2	pointed out	12	announced	22	was
3	was making	13	had	23	instruct
4	asked	14	could	24	not to come
5	had	15	explained	25	had
6	replied	16	was		
7	wasn't	17	would		
8	told	18	declared		
9	to speak	19	was		
10	deny	20	was		

B
1 Sally says (that) Phil's going to phone her tomorrow.
2 Sally, you told me (that) Phil was going to phone you the next day.
3 Nick tells me (that) he passed his driving test last week.
4 Nick, you said (that) you'd passed your driving test the week before.
5 Ken tells me (that) he's sorry, he can't see me and Kate this weekend.
6 Ken told me (that) he was sorry, he couldn't see me and Kate the other weekend.

C
1 where we can buy course books
2 if/whether the school has an internet connection
3 how many students there are in a group
4 how we will be placed in the different levels
5 what time we finish in the afternoon
6 if/whether we can get drinks in the school
7 how I get to the town centre / how to get to the town centre
8 which dictionary we should buy / which dictionary to buy

15 Conditional sentences

A 1 e 2 a 3 f 4 c 5 b

B
1 If you eat all your vegetables, I'll give you some dessert.
2 You will have stomach ache if you eat too many plums.
3 If I help you with your homework, will you do the washing-up?
4 If you don't go to bed now, you will be tired in the morning.
5 Your mother will be cross if you come home late.

C
1 You won't be able to afford a holiday unless you stop buying CDs.
2 She won't go to school tomorrow unless her cold is better.
3 Unless she studies hard, she won't pass the exam.
4 Unless you listen, you won't know what to do.

D
1	won't be	5	won't need	9	won't need
2	don't save	6	go	10	earn
3	stop	7	won't be		
4	will save	8	mends		

E
1 You would enjoy France more, if you could speak better French.
2 If I were you, I would tell him the truth.
3 If my father ate more slowly, he would not get stomach ache.
4 There would be less pollution if people did not fly so much.

F
1 Suzie would live in Beverly Hills if she could live anywhere in the world.
2 probable future event
3 probable future event
4 If the Queen rang, I would be too shocked to speak.
5 If I had a million pounds, I would buy a sports car.
6 probable future event

G
1	would be	9	would	17	talk
2	had	10	were	18	you'll
3	could	11	were	19	won't
4	had	12	I'd	20	it's
5	could	13	I'd	21	don't
6	I'd	14	could	22	think
7	was	15	go		
8	would	16	take		

16 Nouns

A
1	A	7	-	13	The
2	the	8	a	14	-
3	the	9	-	15	the
4	a	10	the	16	the
5	a	11	-	17	-
6	The	12	-	18	the

B

1	much	11	-	21	-
2	hope	12	money	22	weather
3	results	13	-	23	was
4	trips	14	languages	24	a
5	accommodation	15	jobs	25	luck
6	some	16	any	26	jobs
7	information	17	experience	27	many
8	much	18	chance	28	times
9	time	19	news		
10	work	20	was		

C

1	wallpaper	5	washing machine
2	CD player	6	fruit bowl
3	nail file	7	bread knife
4	kitchen door	8	rubber gloves

D

1	cup of coffee	5	matchbox
2	packets of crisps	6	cans of soup
3	teacup	7	jam jar
4	Cola cans	8	teapot

E

1	bus stop	6	girlfriend	11	market street
2	school friend	7	town centre	12	fruit stall
3	summer camp	8	coffee bar	13	credit cards
4	sports teachers	9	shoe shop	14	apple pie
5	tennis coach	10	walking shoes	15	orange juice

WORD FOCUS A confessed B on offer

17 Possessives

A

1	your	5	his	9	His
2	my	6	Her	10	My
3	my	7	their	11	their
4	your	8	her	12	your

B

1	mine	5	my	9	My
2	hers	6	hers	10	mine
3	our	7	our	11	My
4	mine	8	our		

C

1	yours	5	its	9	her
2	hers	6	her	10	Our
3	Whose	7	it's	11	It's
4	mine	8	My	12	your

WORD FOCUS A 1 B 2

D

1 Olivia's history result was better than Jessica's.
2 Ben's history result was better than Daniel's and Joseph's.
3 In general, the girls' history results were better than the boys'.
4 In art, though, the boys' results were better than the girls'.

E

1 *The Age Of Innocence*
2 *Giovanni's Room*
3 *The Magician's Nephew*
4 *Schindler's Ark*
5 *The Corridors Of Power*
6 *The Horse's Mouth*
7 *Towers Of Silence*
8 *On Her Majesty's Secret Service*

F

1	Harry's	7	his	13	your
2	sister's	8	theirs	14	Melanie's
3	hers	9	my	15	Its
4	mine	10	parents'	16	their
5	Yours	11	our	17	my
6	brother's	12	ours		

18 Demonstratives

A

1	this	4	That	7	these
2	those	5	this	8	those
3	this	6	this	9	this

WORD FOCUS A disappointing B dreadful

B

1	that, one	4	this, that, one
2	these, those, ones	5	those, these, ones
3	this, that, one	6	this, that, one

C

1	That's	5	this is	9	This
2	this is	6	that's	10	that
3	That's	7	this		
4	this	8	That's		

D

1	this	4	Those	7	this
2	that	5	that	8	these
3	these	6	That		

E

1	that	6	this	11	These
2	that	7	this	12	those
3	this	8	those	13	this
4	This	9	That	14	this
5	these	10	this	15	this

19 Quantifiers

A

1	a few, any	3	a few, no
2	no, a little	4	a little, any

B

1	Any	7	some	13	no
2	no	8	some	14	any
3	a little	9	any	15	a little
4	any	10	much	16	a lot of
5	a few	11	a few	17	a little
6	any	12	a lot		

C
1	everything	7	anybody	13	everywhere
2	somebody	8	nobody	14	anybody
3	everything	9	something	15	everything
4	anybody	10	somewhere	16	everything
5	anything	11	somebody		
6	something	12	everything		

D
1	a little	7	some	13	a lot of
2	no	8	much	14	any
3	any	9	a lot	15	A few
4	everywhere	10	everything	16	none
5	anything	11	a few		
6	anywhere	12	many		

20 Comparative and superlative forms

A
1 smaller than; the smallest
2 lighter than; the heaviest
3 bigger; than
4 more expensive than; the most expensive

B
1	more settled	4	weaker
2	better than	5	the weakest
3	the best		

C
1 I find Clive more interesting than Tom. His jokes are some of the funniest ones I've ever heard.
2 Greta is better than most people at chess but she isn't the best player in the club.
3 Loïc is the laziest person I've ever met. He does less than anyone else.

D
1 I sing worse than everybody else.
2 Nowadays, she visits us less often than she used to.
3 My mother looks after her plants more carefully than anyone else.
4 Rod arrived earlier than everyone else.

E
1	more	11	the most positive
2	less	12	younger
3	longer than	13	worse
4	the oldest	14	easier
5	more	15	older
6	harder	16	wiser
7	more expensive	17	more relaxed
8	more complicated than	18	more positively
9	the highest	19	better
10	more optimistically		

F
1	further *or* harder	3	earlier
2	higher		

21 (Not) as … as, enough, too

A
1 as much as before
2 understand as well as the other students
3 speak as fluently as them
4 as quickly as you hoped
5 as many lessons as I wanted
6 the same amount of homework as last year
7 the same books as before
8 as easy as the one last year
WORD FOCUS   A progressing   B a challenge

B
1	enough flour	5	fast enough
2	strong enough	6	large enough
3	enough air	7	often enough
4	enough money	8	well enough

C
1	enough time to	4	long enough for
2	enough sausages for	5	warm enough to
3	light enough to	6	loudly enough

D
1	too many	5	too little
2	too young	6	too few
3	too long	7	too well
4	too little		

E
1	enough people	9	too oily
2	as close together as	10	enough time to
3	short enough	11	too big
4	too many	12	loudly enough
5	too much	13	as spectacular as
6	too big	14	too noisy for
7	too cold for	15	too late to
8	as wonderful as	16	big enough for

22 Adverbs

A
1 never sleeps upstairs
2 rarely take their holidays abroad
3 you ever go to bed late
4 often treats the dogs badly
5 Larry usually try hard
6 goes to Scotland every week

B
1 coming to the studio this morning
2 have often been in the news
3 in the papers every day
4 has just come out
5 quietly in a little village
6 occasionally went to London at weekends
7 sometimes went for a walk
8 came to the house twice a week
9 hardly ever spoke
10 happily in a village for a whole year

C
1	a bit	3	fairly	5	quite
2	really	4	very	6	incredibly

D
1	maybe	5	Perhaps	9	definitely
2	definitely	6	maybe	10	maybe
3	probably	7	definitely		
4	definitely	8	certainly		

E
1	at home most years	9	absolutely delighted
2	are usually	10	certainly made
3	definitely prefer	11	quite fluently
4	often been	12	rather different
5	to Spain last year	13	absolutely enormous
6	very big	14	particularly attractive
7	on the coast in the summer	15	certainly want
8	practically empty	16	will probably

23 Connecting adverbs

A
1	too	5	either
2	either	6	neither
3	so	7	so
4	too	8	too

B
1	Neither did I	4	So do I	7	So did I
2	So is mine	5	Neither do I	8	So did I
3	Neither do I	6	So do I	9	so do I

C
1	Neither are mine	5	Her brother does, too
2	I have, too	6	Isabel can't either
3	So do I	7	so did his older sister
4	So is his sister	8	Neither does his brother

D
1	only	3	even
2	only	4	Even

E
1	actually	3	hopefully	5	luckily
2	Apparently	4	obviously		

F
1	Neither	5	finally	9	then
2	Hopefully	6	first	10	obviously
3	even	7	Hopefully	11	unfortunately
4	Meanwhile	8	too	12	either

24 Prepositions (1)

A
1	out of; at	3	to; by; on	5	in; in; at
2	to; on; in	4	in; with	6	by; in

B
1	by	3	down	5	At
2	by	4	on	6	over

C
1	on offer	3	In the end	5	at home
2	out of stock	4	by credit card	6	in cash

D
1	to	5	to/towards	9	of
2	to	6	on	10	with
3	from	7	with	11	about
4	for	8	for	12	with

WORD FOCUS   A   no wonder

E
1	into town	6	polite to	11	on the way
2	interested in	7	on the corner	12	responsible for
3	reason for	8	happy about	13	advice on
4	different from	9	by bike	14	on holiday
5	ready for	10	effect on		

25 Prepositions (2)

A
1	in the middle of	4	at the front of
2	in front of	5	on top of
3	at the top of		

B
1	In line with	4	at the bottom of
2	in case	5	in view of
3	in touch with	6	On behalf of

C
1	in charge of	4	at first	7	in the middle of
2	As a result of	5	in return for	8	in love with
3	on top of	6	in the end	9	at the end of

D
1	of	3	to	5	to
2	in	4	in		

E
1	In fact	4	in the meantime
2	for example	5	thanks to
3	at night	6	in a hurry

F
1	In conclusion	3	on time
2	Due to	4	in the morning

26 Linking words

A
1	either … or	3	both … and	5	either … or
2	neither … nor	4	either … or		

B
1	either	5	for	9	either
2	or	6	both	10	or
3	neither	7	and	11	because
4	nor	8	because	12	because

C
1	so many people that	5	so hot that
2	so cold that	6	so little money left that
3	so much noise that	7	so salty that
4	such a hot day that	8	such salty food that

D
1	in order to	6	both	11	because
2	so much that	7	and	12	in order to
3	Because	8	such	13	such
4	so that	9	either		
5	for	10	or		

27 Linking sentences

A
1 unless 4 unless
2 in case 5 unless
3 unless

B
1 the boxes are kept in a dry place
2 the goods are not in perfect condition
3 we hear from you within a week
4 they are in good condition
5 customers do not have an appointment

C
1 my husband in case he wondered where I was
2 an umbrella in case it rains later
3 down the name of the film in case you forget it
4 some more food in case Tina comes for dinner
5 you a map in case you can't / aren't able to find the hotel

D
1 Although Brian is quite young, his work is greatly appreciated.
2 Brian is quite young. However, his work is greatly appreciated. / His work, however, is greatly appreciated.
3 Mary is a favourite with the boss but her colleagues don't like her.
4 Although Mary is a favourite with the boss, her colleagues don't like her.
5 Mary is a favourite with the boss. However, her colleagues don't like her. / Her colleagues, however, don't like her.
6 Joan's English is not very good. However, she gets her message across.
7 Joan's English is not very good. She gets her message across, though. / Though Joan's English is not very good, she gets her message across.
8 Tony always arrives late but he usually finishes his work on time.
9 Although Tony always arrives late, he usually finishes his work on time.

WORD FOCUS B

E
1 What's more 7 though
2 However 8 On the other hand
3 unless 9 if
4 though 10 However
5 Moreover 11 unless
6 in case 12 What's more

28 Relative clauses

A
1 who/that 5 whose 9 who/that
2 whose 6 which/that 10 which/that
3 who/that 7 who/that
4 which/that 8 which/that

B
1 which/that cost
2 which/that my cousin bought
3 who/that works with
4 whose parents were
5 which/that thieves burgled
6 whose house thieves burgled
7 who/that saved a child
8 whose photo was

C
1 Virginia Woolf, whose sister was a painter, wrote *A Room of One's Own*, which deals with the difficulties for women in a man's world.
2 In 1958 Rosalind Franklin, who helped to discover the structure of DNA, died of cancer, which in those days was incurable.
3 Grantham, which lies in Lincolnshire, is famous as the birthplace of Margaret Thatcher, who was British Prime MInister for 11 years.
4 'Imagine', which is still a very popular song, was written by John Lennon, who died in 1980.

D
1 Sara read War and Peace in just two weeks
2 his car
3 the Lake District
4 The manager accused Bill of stealing

E
1 , which 5 , which/that 9 which/that
2 which/that 6 , whose 10 which/that/-
3 , who 7 , which
4 which/that 8 , which

29 Expressions of time, place, and reason

A
1 She arrived at school by 8.45.
2 She played basketball after her history lesson.
3 She didn't get home until 4.30.
4 After Maria finished her homework, she watched television.
5 She was watching television when her mother came home.
6 Her brother told a couple of jokes while her father was washing the dishes.
7 Her father went to bed after he had washed the dishes.

B
1 until 3 as soon as 5 until
2 After 4 while 6 when

C
1 when 3 where 5 why
2 where 4 when

D
1 when 4 whenever 7 whenever
2 where 5 wherever
3 when 6 why

E

1	when	6	where	11	when
2	when	7	whenever	12	By
3	where	8	As soon as	13	wherever
4	while	9	while		
5	until	10	why		

WORD FOCUS A turned up OR appeared from nowhere
B guarding

30 Leaving out words

A

1	Free from 11 to 12	6	I will lead the meeting
2	doctor's surgery	7	and can you send
3	he will have to	8	send an update
4	have to talk about them first	9	can do
5	would you like to lead the meeting	10	I'll order some coffee

B

1	wondered	5	follows the lives of three families
2	he has	6	witty
3	finishes	7	it is
4	three centuries	8	you must

C

1 was very talented
2 I didn't like the fact
3 but it didn't annoy me
4 I wasn't planning to have another drink
5 I will have another drink
6 I can't have another drink
7 Do you really have to go?
8 Well, I should go
9 he probably expects me to go to bed early as well

D

1	standing	5	photographed
2	moving	6	sitting
3	married	7	wearing
4	mentioned	8	talking

E

1	the man behind	5	the woman between
2	the woman next to	6	Nick.
3	the woman in front of	7	Behind Molly.
4	the man next to	8	Jenny.

F

1 Pele is the footballer often described as the greatest of all time.
2 James Earl Jones is an actor best known as the voice of Darth Vader in the *Star Wars* films.
3 I passed the message to the policeman waiting outside the door.
4 The finest bananas in the world are grown in Madagascar.
5 Computers built in China are cheaper than British ones.
6 Apples bought from a greengrocer's usually taste better than supermarket apples.

Answer key Over to you

01 Present simple and present continuous

- Dear Olivia
  My name is Antonio. I live in Madrid with my family.
  I have two brothers and one sister. My sister is older
  than me and she works in the local library - she reads
  all the time! My brothers are both younger than me
  and they're still at school. My father is a doctor and my
  mother works at home. I go to university in the centre of
  Madrid and I study French and English. In the evenings
  I often go to the cinema with my friends, or eat out at
  a restaurant with them. We love Chinese food! Tell me
  a bit about yourself too! What do you do, and do you
  enjoy living in London?
  Best wishes,
  Antonio
- I'm sitting on the sand at the beach. Kelly is lying
  next to me and she's reading a fashion magazine and
  listening to her MP3 player. A man is walking his dog.
  How funny, the dog ran into the waves and now he's
  shaking himself and making the man completely wet
  too! A boy is flying a kite with his friend - it's a huge kite
  and is flying right above our heads! Some people are
  swimming in the sea and others are playing volleyball
  on the beach.
- I'm sorry, I can't go shopping with you on Saturday
  because I'm going swimming with Petra. / I'm sorry, I
  can't play football with you on Thursday because I'm
  watching television with Sonya. / I'm sorry, I can't go to
  the cinema with you on Monday because I'm having
  dinner with Michael.

02 Talking about the past

- When I was 11, I won a dancing competition. / When I
  was 19, I climbed Mont Blanc. / When I was 25, I ran a
  marathon.
- When I heard about the attack, I was eating my lunch at
  work and looking at a news website on the internet. The
  sun was shining outside and there were a lot of people
  walking in the street below my office. My brother was
  sitting on the bus, reading a book, and listening to the
  radio on his phone. We both heard the news at the
  same time.
- I used to play hockey on Saturdays. / I used to visit my
  grandparents every week. / I used to believe in Santa
  Claus.

03 Present perfect

- I've ridden a camel in the desert. / I've swum with
  dolphins. / I've eaten oysters.
- Robin has never climbed a mountain. / He has never
  broken his arm. / He has never been skiing.
- I've always had brown hair. / I've always liked
  football. / I've always played the piano.
- I've been sitting in this classroom for 20 minutes. / I've
  been learning English since 2006. / I've been reading
  this book for two weeks.

04 Past simple and present perfect; past perfect

- When I got back home, everything was in a complete
  mess. My first thought was what on earth had the
  dog been up to. I soon found out. He had eaten my
  clothes and chewed my slippers. He had pulled down
  the curtains and he had knocked over the TV! There
  was water all over the floor in the living room because
  the dog had run into the coffee table and the vase of
  flowers on the top had fallen over. The vase had broken
  too so there was glass on the floor. It was lucky that the
  dog hadn't hurt himself!
- Have you had any breakfast today? ~ Yes, I have. I had
  two pieces of toast.
  Did you have breakfast yesterday? ~ No, I didn't have
  enough time.
  Have you done your homework today? ~ No, I haven't
  done it yet.
  Did you do your homework yesterday? ~ Yes, I did it
  after the football match.
  Have you watched television today? ~ No, I haven't. I've
  listened to the radio, though. Did you watch television
  yesterday? ~ Yes, I watched an old James Bond film after
  dinner.

05 The future

- I'm going to go whitewater rafting in Colorado. I'm
  going to fly from Heathrow to Chicago. Then I'm going
  to take the coach to Colorado and I'm going to stay in a
  chalet in the forest. I'm going to stay for a whole week.
  I'm going to do their safety training for the first two
  days, and then I'm going to go on the rapids with an
  instructor. It's going to be so exciting!
- In the next fifty years, we'll have flying cars. There will
  be cities on the moon and people will be able to go into
  space on holiday.
- I'll tidy my bedroom room. Shall I do the washing-up
  and take the rubbish out? I'll do the vacuuming in the
  living room.

06 Ability, permission, and requests

- When I was younger, I couldn't swim, but now I can swim 30 lengths. / When I was younger, I couldn't speak any English, but now I can speak a little. / When I was younger, I couldn't afford new gadgets, but now I can buy whatever I want.
- When I finish my studies, I'll be able to get a job. / When I finish my studies, I'll be able to buy my own house. / When I finish my studies, I'll be able to speak English perfectly!
- Would you pass me the salt? ~ Of course. Can you pass me the ketchup, please? ~ Here you are. Please can you pour some water? ~ No problem. Would you give me a napkin? ~ Of course.

07 Possibility and probability; perfect modals

- He may have forgotten about our meeting. / He might have missed the bus. / He could be lost.
- After I've finished my studies at school, I may go to university. I might get a job, or I could travel around the world.
- There must have been thousands of people working on the pyramids because they're so large and they must have used elephants, because the stones are too heavy to carry. They can't have used machines, because they hadn't been invented.

08 Duty and obligation

- You shouldn't panic. You should try to make the house secure and then you should call the police. You ought to make a list of everything that has been stolen, but you shouldn't upset yourself. You probably ought to tell your neighbour too, and you should ask them if they saw anything strange today. If you feel nervous, you should ask if they can sit with you for a while.
- A zookeeper has to feed and clean the animals. / A policeman has to wear a uniform. He has to catch criminals. / A nurse has to wear a uniform, and she has to look after people who are ill.

09 Infinitives and -ing forms (1)

- I liked shopping on Oxford Street and I particularly liked looking for bargains in the sales. I didn't enjoy going round Buckingham Palace - it was boring, but at the same time I liked imagining that I was walking where the Queen had walked before! I enjoyed visiting London Zoo and seeing the animals most.
- I will encourage my child to play an instrument because I think it's important to have hobbies that are creative. I will teach him to speak French so he can learn about another culture. I want him to be a doctor so I will persuade him to go to university and encourage him to work very hard!

10 Infinitives and -ing forms (2)

- I am afraid of swimming - I can't swim! I'm excited about parachuting but I'm a bit nervous too because I'm scared of heights! I'm not interested in writing poetry and I find it difficult to have creative ideas. I'm tired of reading because it always takes me so long to finish a book. I like reading comics, though. I'm terrible at skiing and fell over all the time when I went last year.

11 The passive

- *The Importance Of Being Ernest* was written by Oscar Wilde. / The Sydney Opera House was designed by Jorn Utzon. / The telephone was invented by Alexander Graham Bell. / The Eiffel Tower was designed by Gustave Eiffel. / *The Deer Hunter* was directed by Michael Cimino. / The ceiling of the Sistine Chapel was painted by Michelangelo. / *The Lord Of The Rings* was written by J.R.R. Tolkien.
- I would have the town centre pedestrianized. / I would have the buses painted yellow. / I would have the streets cleaned.

12 Phrasal and prepositional verbs

- give up - I gave up smoking last year.
  make up - That word doesn't exist - you made it up!
  look up - I looked up the meaning of the word 'prole-tariat' in the dictionary.
- check in - I arrived at the hotel at 3p.m. and checked in.
  take in - I'm sorry, that's too much for me to take in.
  stand in - Peter couldn't play football on Saturday, so his friend Mark had to stand in.
- move on - I couldn't answer the first question, so I moved on to the second.
  turn on - I turned on the lights in the kitchen.
  try on - She tried the shirt on before she bought it.

13 Indirect speech (1)

- The two men said they would meet at the bank at 3 p.m. Pat told Ted to bring a gun and said that he would bring masks so no one would see their faces. He told Ted to wear black clothes and gloves. Ted said that they would need a getaway car. He asked if Pat knew where to find one and Pat said that he did. They said they would take the money to a warehouse outside town and take the car to a quiet road in the countryside and leave it there.

14 Indirect speech (2)

- I told my friend to turn right when he came out of the station. I told him to go past the post office. I warned him not to take the second turning on the left. I reminded him to take the third turning and to look for my green front door. He was so confused, though, that in the end I agreed to pick him up at the station!

15 Conditional sentences

- If I don't pass my exams, I won't be able to go to university. / If I fail my driving test, I won't be able to visit my friends in Scotland. / If I don't pay my bills on time, I will have to pay a fine.
- If I were taller, I would be a policeman. / If I lived in a big house, I would invite my friends to dinner. / If I had more money, I would buy a nice car.

16 Nouns

- I have a reading lamp on top of the bookshelf. I keep a glass vase on the window sill. There is a hairdryer in the bedroom. I keep a gold watch in a chest of drawers. There are milk bottles in the fridge. I keep the toothpaste in the bathroom. I always put the dog food in the cupboard next to the dog basket. I have a teapot and a coffee pot in the kitchen.

17 Possessives

- My favourite hobby's reading and my brother's is fishing. His hobby is more expensive than mine because he has to buy more things. / My parents have a plasma TV in the living room. Their TV is bigger than mine. / My friend Sara has an Xbox. Mine is better than hers and my games are more exciting than hers.

18 Demonstratives

- Do you like this shirt? ~ Not really. I prefer that blue one. I think blue suits you more than green. Why don't you try this light blue one with those jeans? ~ OK, I will. And what do you think about those black shoes over there? ~ I think these shoes are nicer because they look more expensive. Those shoes are very small too.

19 Quantifiers

- In my fridge, I have some butter, a little cheese, a tomato, a lot of lettuce and some milk. I have no water and I don't have many eggs. I need to buy some ham and some water and I want to buy some yoghurts too.
- Everybody at the company earns over £25,000. Everyone must wear a suit, but no one worries about wearing a tie. Everyone is very friendly and they welcome new people, so no one is unhappy!
- I'm looking for somebody who can speak German and is well-organized. I'd like to give the job to somebody who is intelligent and calm. I'm not looking for anybody who is lazy or for anybody who panics under pressure!

20 Comparative and superlative forms

- Usain Bolt is the fastest sprinter in the world. He is faster than Carl Lewis. / Everest is the highest mountain in the world. It is higher than Mont Blanc. / Burj Dubai in Dubai, UAE, is the tallest building in the world. It is taller than the Chrysler Building.
- My life is easier than my grandparents'. Clothes and food are less expensive. Houses are bigger. Cars are faster. My grandparents had to start work when they were younger than I am now, and it was more important for the family that they earned money straight away. Perhaps I'm luckier than they were, because I'm going to be able to go to university.

21 (Not) as … as, enough, too

- The music was too loud and there were too many people, so I couldn't hear what people were saying and there wasn't enough room for everyone to sit down. / There wasn't enough food so I was really hungry! / The party wasn't as good as Sam's party last week and it didn't go on as long as her party did. I didn't know all the people there and most of them weren't as much fun as my friends.
- You are too young / You aren't old enough. / The US is too far away. / We don't have enough money to pay for the flight. / It's too expensive.

22 Adverbs

- Break two eggs carefully into a bowl.
  Gently pour in some milk.
  Mix the eggs and milk thoroughly.
  Melt some butter slowly in a pan and add the egg mixture.
  Meanwhile cut two slices of bread and put them in the toaster. Toast them lightly and then spread them thinly with butter.
  Stir the eggs quickly but carefully and pour the egg mixture carefully on the toast.

23 Connecting adverbs

- First, we need to find some flat ground. ~ Yes, then we should unpack the tents. ~ How do we put them up? ~ Actually, I'm not sure. Unfortunately, I've never put up a tent before. ~ Luckily, I have, and it's very easy. First, we put the poles together … ~ OK, you take charge of the tents. Meanwhile, I'll start a fire.

24 Prepositions (1)

- Spider-Man: At the beginning of the film, Peter Parker is a normal schoolboy, but he is tired of being bullied by other kids. At the museum, he is bitten by a spider and he becomes a superhero. He is astonished by his new powers. He finds that criminals are afraid of him, but his girlfriend is angry with him because he is never at home. The millionaire Norman Osborn is jealous of Spider-Man's powers and becomes the Green Goblin.

25 Prepositions (2)

- There is a painting on the wall in front of me. Behind me, there is a mirror. In the middle of the room, there is a rug. There is a table in the corner, and there is a computer on the table.
- My father used to work in the city, but now he works from home. In other words, he's self-employed. He used to hate the journey to work - he was always late because of the terrible traffic, and had a bad back, thanks to sitting in an office all day. He was always in a hurry, and never got home in time for dinner. He didn't sleep well at night, and in the morning he was always grumpy.

26 Linking words

- The TorchBreadknife is an amazing gadget: it is both a breadknife and a torch. You can use it either at home or outside. You can use it for slicing bread, and it includes a torch so that you don't have to worry if the lights go out. Buy one now, because you never know when you might need to slice bread in the dark.

27 Linking sentences

- If we don't stop cutting down the forests, the ozone layer will disappear. The seas will continue to rise unless we stop polluting the atmosphere. Moreover, many endangered species will die out if we don't stop destroying their homes . We should start to think about using solar power in case the fossil fuels run out.
- Some people claim to have seen UFOs, but we have no proof that they come from other planets. There are millions of other planets, so there must be life on some of them. However, there is no water on any of them. On the other hand, we don't know if aliens need water.

28 Relative clauses

- William Shakespeare is the man who wrote *Romeo And Juliet* and many other famous plays. / J.K. Rowling is the woman who wrote the Harry Potter books. / Bill Gates is the man who owns Microsoft. / Charles Babbage is the man who invented the first computer. / George Lucas is the man who directed/wrote *Star Wars*.
- Paris, which is the capital of France and is France's largest city, is situated on the river Seine. The main shopping street, which is called the Champs Elysees, is one of the most famous streets in the world. The Eiffel Tower, which was originally temporary, was built in 1889 for an exhibition and is perhaps the most famous monument in Paris. The Arc de Triomphe, which is at the top of the Champs Élysées, is 50 m tall.

29 Expressions of time, place, and reason

- Do you remember when we were 16 and we sneaked out of our houses to go to the nightclub? ~ Oh yes. I waited until my parents were asleep, then I climbed out of the bedroom window. ~ And as soon as my mum went to bed, while my dad was watching TV, I crept out of the back door. ~ Then we met at the top of the street and we were at the club by 11 p.m.

30 Leaving out words

- When I was younger, I couldn't speak English, but now I can. / When I was younger, I believed in Santa Claus, but now I don't. / When I was younger, it was expensive to travel by plane, but now it isn't.

Index

My notes